INSIGHT *Pocket* GUIDES

London

P9-APC-769

APA PUBLICATIONS

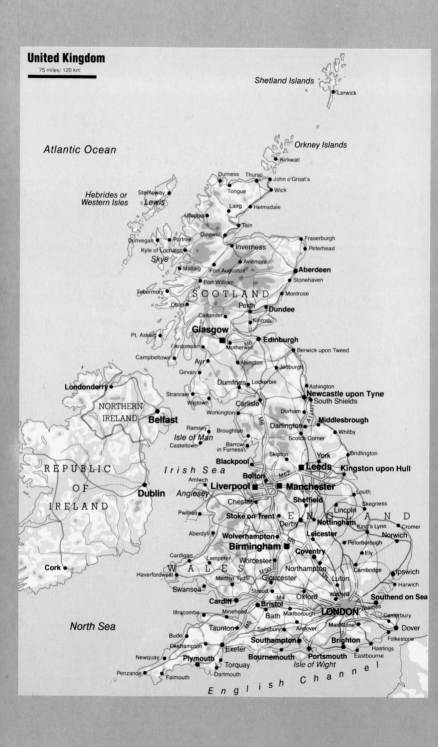

United Kingdom

75 miles/ 120 km

Shetland Islands
• Lerwick

Atlantic Ocean

Orkney Islands
• Kirkwall

Hebrides or
Western Isles
Lewis
• Stornoway
Durness Thurso John o'Groat's
Tongue • Wick
Lairg Helmsdale
Ullapool
Tain
Dingwall Fraserburgh
Dunvegan Portree Inverness Peterhead
Kyle of Lochalsh
Skye Aviemore
• Mallaig Fort Augustus Aberdeen
Fort William Stonehaven
Tobermory
SCOTLAND Montrose
Oban Perth Dundee
Callander Kinross
Pt. Askaig Glasgow Edinburgh
Ardrossan M8 Motherwell
Campbeltown Berwick upon Tweed
Ayr Abington
Girvan Jedburgh
Londonderry • Dumfries Lockerbie Ashington
Stranraer Newcastle upon Tyne
NORTHERN Wigtown Carlisle South Shields
IRELAND Workington Durham Middlesbrough
Belfast M6 Darlington Whitby
Ramsey Broughton Scotch Corner
Isle of Man Barrow Skipton Bridlington
Castletown in Furness York
REPUBLIC Blackpool Kingston upon Hull
Irish Sea Bolton Leeds
OF Amlwch Liverpool Manchester Louth
Anglesey Sheffield Skegness
IRELAND Chester Lincoln
Pwllheli Stoke on Trent ENGLAND Cromer
Dublin Derby Nottingham King's Lynn
Aberdyfi Wolverhampton Leicester Norwich
Cork Birmingham Coventry Peterborough
Cardigan Lampeter Worcester Ely
Haverfordwest Merthyr Tydfil M50 Northampton Cambridge Ipswich
WALES Gloucester Luton Harwich
Swansea Stroud Oxford Watford Southend on Sea
Cardiff Bristol M4 Thames Canterbury
Ilfracombe Minehead Bath Marlborough LONDON
North Sea Taunton Salisbury Andover Maidstone Dover
Bude Southampton Brighton Folkestone
Okehampton Exeter Bournemouth Portsmouth Hastings
Newquay Plymouth Torquay Isle of Wight Eastbourne
Penzance Falmouth Dartmouth
English Channel

Dear Visitor!

Buckingham Palace, the British Museum, Oxford Street, St Paul's… London is a roll call of top attractions, a city that is steeped in history and yet constantly changing. Whether this is your first visit, or your one hundredth, you'll discover a city that has undergone a long-awaited renewal. This guide is your compass for the streets of London.

In these pages two of Insight's correspondents will help enrich your experience of the city. Culled from different generations, they present a London that is a fascinating metropolis of both past and present.

 Roland Collins is a writer and historian, and has lived in the city for longer than he cares to remember. His main interest is in social history, but he is also an accomplished artist with London exhibitions. Now based in a tiny square just off Tottenham Court Road, he says fondly of the city: 'We've been married for over 60 years. She isn't the girl I swapped vows with, but we are still very much in love.' This loves shines through the walking suggestions that he has put together.

 Beverly Harper is also a massive enthusiast for everything London. Harper is Insight's correspondent for London's all-consuming passions: shopping, eating out and nightlife. She also writes about such subjects for London's own magazine, Time Out, and the Sunday Times. Harper is well-schooled in both the trendy and the perennial in this great city, and she has selected something of both for you. We hope that her tips will help you to enjoy tasting, seeing and experiencing the essence of London.

Hans Höfer
Publisher, Insight Guides

C O N T E N T S

Pages 2/3:
View from
Waterloo Bridge

Pages 10/11: Close-up of Houses of Parliament

London

320m / 0.2 miles

To Hampstead and Camden Town
To Paddington Station
To Notting Hill Gate and Portobello Road
To Harrods and Brompton Oratory
To Chelsea and King's Road

Inner Circle
Open Air Theatre
Inner Circle
Bedford College
Mme. Tussaud's
Academy of Music
Outer Circle
Walk Rd.
Harley St.
Portland St.
Devonshire
Weymouth
New
Wimpole St.
Cavendish Place
BBC
Wallace Collection
Outer Circle
Albany St.
Stanhope St.
Circle
Hampstead Rd.
Euston Tower
Holy Trinity
Cleveland St.
Titchfield St.
Fitzroy St.
Post Office Tower
Charlotte St.
Rathbone St.

Eversholt St.
St. Pancras Station
King's Cross Station
Euston Station
Euston Rd.
Euston Rd.
Mabledon Pl.
Judd St.
Argyll St.
Swinton St.
Gray's Inn Rd.
Square
Place
Coram Fields
University College
Tavistock
University
BLOOMSBURY
Gower St.
Montague St.
Southampton Row
Guildford St.
Millman St.
Lamb's Conduit St.
Red Lion St.
Russell St.
Great
New
Oxford St.
ST. GILES
British Museum
Court Rd.
Tottenham

Selfridges
MAYFAIR
Oxford St.
Brook St.
Roosevelt Memorial
Grosvenor St.
New Bond Street
Old Bond Street
North Audley St.
Park St.
Park Lane
Park Lane
Hyde Park
Park Lane
Achilles
Apsley House
Knightsbridge
Wellington Arch
Grosvenor
Belgrave Square
Belgrave Place
Ecclestone St.
BELGRAVIA
Regent St.
St.
St.
Palladium
Regent St.
SOHO
Wardour St.
Shaftesbury
Greek St.
Leicester Square
Charing Cross Rd.
Av.
Freemasons Hall
Kingsway
Royal Opera House
Covent Garden
Strand
K
Museum of Mankind
Royal Academy
Piccadilly
Piccadilly Circus
Regent St.
Haymarket
National Portrait Gallery
National Gallery
Trafalgar Square
St. Martin-in-the-Fields
Charing Cross Station
Northumberland Av.
Strand
Somerset House
Victoria
Cleopatra's Needle
Queen Elizabeth Hall
Embankment
St. James's St.
St. James's Square
ICA
Mall
Whitehall
Admiralty
Banqueting House
Royal Festival Hall
Piccadilly
Green Park
St. James's Palace
Marlborough House
The Mall
St. James's Park
Government Offices
County Hall
Lancaster House
Constitution Hill
Wellington
Buckingham Palace
Palace
Gardens
Queen's Gallery
Royal Mews
Buckingham Palace Rd.
Victoria Station
Victoria St.
Queen Victoria Memorial
Birdcage Walk
Wellington Barracks
New Scotland Yard
Victoria St.
Westminster Cathedral
George St.
Westminster Abbey
Victoria St.
Peter St.
Millbank
Westminster Bridge
Houses of Parliament
Thames
St.
Lambeth Bridge
St. Thomas Hospital
Lambeth Palace
Lambeth Pl. Rd.
Lambeth Rd.

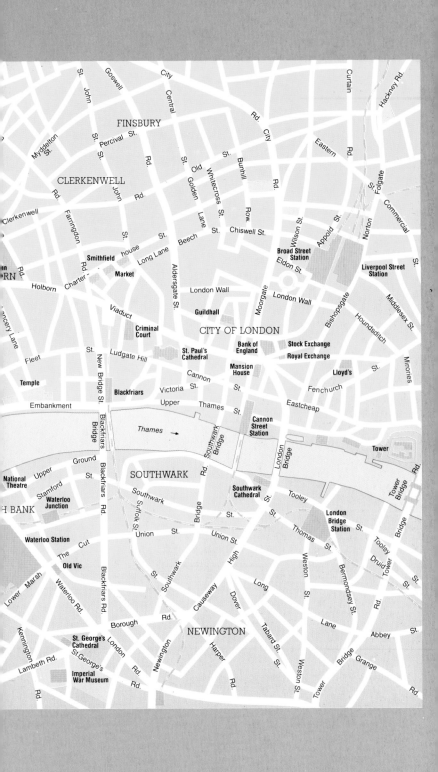

HISTORY

Act One: A Hill and a River

Standing above the Thames on Tower Hill are the surprisingly substantial remains of Londinium, the city established 2,000 years ago by thrusting empire builders from southern Europe, the Romans under Claudius. They imposed a civilisation where none existed before, lighting a lamp in the Celtic darkness.

In Trinity Square a section of the wall the Romans built to defend their city still dominates, the survivor of centuries of neglect and destruction. Elsewhere the wall is threaded through the fabric of Victorian development or buried below modern street levels. It was certainly a necessary protection. As the capital of Britannia, as

Artist's impression of Roman Londinium

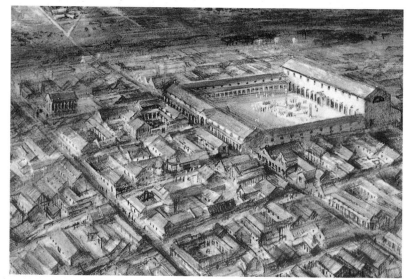

Roman Britain was called, London had its complement of imposing public buildings, and the excavated remains of the finest are on display at the Museum of London (see Walk 4: *Tower and City*).

Towards the end of the 3rd century London was beginning to be affected by the situation overseas culminating in the withdrawal of the Roman garrison in 410 in the face of attacks by the hordes of northern Europe. The fabric of both buildings and society crumbled, but after this hiccup in its development, the city once again rose to importance under the Saxons.

Light in the Dark Ages

Not for 200 years is there any

written reference to London until St Augustine was sent to establish a bishopric and the first St Paul's Cathedral was founded by Ethelbert. Little remains that mirrors Anglo-Saxon building skills, though there is ample evidence in the Sutton Hoo ship burial in the British Museum of their considerable craftsmanship.

In spite of an early defeat of the Danes by Alfred, King of Wessex, and his foresight in repairing the Roman walls, London eventually succumbed to the invaders. Sweyn, and later Canute, were crowned here in their palace at Aldermanbury. After the accession of Edward the Confessor in 1042 the Court moved to Westminster, and the rebuilding of the 10th-century abbey was begun. From then on kings were crowned, married and buried there.

William the Conqueror's defeat of the Saxons in 1066 was to

'The Frozen Thames' by Abraham Hondius

prove more than a military achievement: the Conquest introduced a culture that was to transform a nation's art and architecture, literature and laws. William's building programme put priority on defence. His White Tower, the building at the core of the Tower of London, was completed by 1097, its monolithic bulk diminished since by walls and bastions and the addition of designer cupolas. A new St Paul's was begun following a fire in 1097, and Westminster Hall in the Palace of Westminster was started 10 years later.

Bursting at the Seams

Under the Normans, London rapidly developed as a centre of trade and, over the next two centuries, the City of London evolved its characteristic pattern of narrow streets and alleys. Inside the walls crowded London's 25,000 people, accommodated in timber-framed houses, worshipping in over 100 parish churches, shopping for meat and fish in the Stocks Market where the Mansion House now stands, and for poultry, bread and milk where today's street names still remind us of the great open-air market that was Cheapside. One public building of the early 1400s survives, though substantially patched, re-roofed and re-fronted, to remind us by its size and importance of the measures taken by the city's merchants to protect their trade interests – the Guildhall, seat of city government and principal meeting place.

West of the city the legal profession organised itself into Inns of Court, having something of the character of university colleges, in the Temple, Lincoln's Inn, Clifford's Inn and Gray's Inn north of Holborn. The Inns of Court probably had Chaucer as a student. By 1389 the author of *The Canterbury Tales* was Clerk of the King's Works in a city of 50,000 inhabitants. No doubt the Black Death of 1348 succeeded where the authorities had failed in limiting the city's alarming growth. Enforcement had proved ineffectual and London had grown well beyond the original walls.

Reading, Writing, Building

The spread of literacy echoed the swelling population. A former apprentice to a London mercer, William Caxton set up a press in Westminster, in 1476, and with royal patronage printed about 80 books, *The Canterbury Tales* and *Morte d'Arthur* among them. His work was carried on in Fleet Street by Wynkyn de Worde, who printed the first book in English and unknowingly started the Street's connection with the dissemination of popular culture through the newspaper.

In architecture Henry VII had begun, at Westminster in 1503, the first complete chapel in the Late Perpendicular style, damned with faint praise by the great architect, Sir Christopher Wren, as 'embroidery' work, but nevertheless a masterpiece. It was Henry's son Henry VIII, however, who was to bring the furthest reaching changes to London. Following the breach with Rome, Henry set about demolishing the power of the Pope in England, and incidentally producing resources for his lavish private spending. The Dissolution of the Monasteries in 1536 brought him revenue and property he could sell or make presents of to close supporters. The city's monastic houses were soon replaced by private dwellings. A hospital gave way to St James's Palace; Charterhouse to a mansion for Lord North. Cardinal Wolsey's house became the nucleus of Whitehall Palace. The Abbey lands of Hyde Park became a deer-park.

London's 'Golden Age'

England entered its 'Golden Age' with the accession of Queen Elizabeth I in 1558. If it was the greatest era in English history then it was the greatest in London's too, and one man, a Londoner by adoption, made an outstanding contribution – William Shakespeare.

Banned from performing his plays in the City he joined another playwright, Ben Jonson, in setting up his playhouse on the south bank of the river opposite St Paul's, alongside the bear pits and brothels that shared the duty of satisfying the Londoner's great desire for entertainment. The thatch-topped theatres-in-the-round, the Hope, the Rose and the Globe, live on only in the names of streets and alleys on Bankside, but a potent and long standing tradition promises that we will soon see actors strutting the boards again in the new Globe.

Lincoln's Inn, home of the law

St Paul's Cathedral

Under Elizabeth I, London's first planning laws were introduced in an attempt to discourage speculative building, as the population shot up from around 50,000 in 1530 to 225,000 by the end of the 16th century. The laws were not obeyed and former monastic lands and gardens became choked with shoddy tenements

If Elizabeth was a hard act to follow, her successor, James I, at least made an educated choice in Inigo Jones as his Surveyor to the King's Works. Jones, in his interpretations of the Italian architect Palladio's purity of style, brought a unique vision all his own to his designs for the Queen's House at Greenwich, a building which must have seemed outrageous at the time. The Banqueting House in Whitehall, in which London was first introduced to Portland stone, and the Queen's Chapel in St James's remain to confirm the trail-blazing character of these major works. In Covent Garden he laid out the prototype of that most typical feature of the city's urban landscape, the London square, though it has been savaged by the later intrusion of the Market and the loss of its arcaded houses. His promised 'handsomest barn in England', St Paul's church, still dominates the western side.

The Queen's House, now the Maritime Museum at Greenwich

Plague and Fire

In 1665 the Great Plague did what no amount of legislation had been able to achieve – restricted London's population: 100,000 people died and were bundled into plague pits. A year later the City was ravaged by fire from the Tower to the Temple, destroying 13,200 houses, 87 parish churches, and the halls of 44 livery companies. Gothic St Paul's was so badly damaged as to make repair impossible.

The rich people never returned to the City, and the drift to the westward suburbs grew as landowners like the Duke of Bedford made their estates available for development. However, the aldermen of the City of London, no doubt activated by self-interest, accepted the challenge that renewal presented, and on Christopher Wren, Surveyor General to the Crown, fell the task of rebuilding. His difficulty

Regent's Park Crescent

lay in presenting proposals acceptable to conflicting interests. Wren's imaginative scheme for Paris-like boulevards radiating from a Place de la Concorde, with a wide riverside quay replacing the huddle of wharves, was abandoned in the face of strong demands for houses, shops and workshops.

Phoenix City

So, opportunity lost, London rose again in the same street pattern, but to the cathedral and parish churches, of which he rebuilt no less than 50, Wren brought an outstanding creativity. These churches, often on cramped or irregular sites, each one signalled by a tower or steeple, and each with its own unique personality, are the principal architectural glory of the City to this day, though their numbers have been decimated by destruction and disuse. St Paul's, hen to the chickens, was started in 1675 and became the acknowledged masterpiece of a man who was 40 when he presented his first design and 79 when the cathedral was finally accepted as finished by Parliament.

Meanwhile, speculative building was transforming the sites of the old mansions and private gardens between the Strand and the river, as well as Holborn, Soho, and, further out, Mayfair and St James's.

Sunset on the Houses of Parliament

Only the railings of Hyde Park could halt the tide of bricks and mortar joining London with the village of Kensington.

With the 18th century, London was beginning to take on a new look characterised by the pattern of streets and squares in Bloomsbury and Mayfair. In the City, the Mansion House was built as an official residence for the Lord Mayor across from a new Palladian home for the Bank of England. The Guildhall gained a new façade, and imposing new hospitals like St Bartholomew's were built.

Whitehall had Government thrust upon it. The palace deserted by the Court was replaced with the public buildings which line it today. Barracks for the Horse Guards were followed by the Admiralty, where the Lords lived next to, if not over, the offices, and the Treasury moved to the site of the Tudor cockpit. The Navy Office found a rather detached existence in the new Somerset House designed by Sir William Chambers.

How the Other Half Lived

In 1801, at the first count of heads, Londoners numbered nearly a million. These inhabitants were beginning to desert the City and crowd into Westminster and Holborn, St Marylebone and St Pancras and across the river into Southwark, Lambeth and Bermondsey. London turned its back on the East End. With its origins in ragged development along the river through Wapping and along the roads to Essex, the East End became the natural point of arrival for foreigners in flight from persecution. They brought their own skills and trades: the Huguenots brought silk weaving to Spitalfields; the Jews from Russia and Poland brought boot and shoe making, clothing and furniture making to the area east of Aldgate. The situation was aggravated by the construction of the docks which swept away whole parishes. In 1825 St Katharine's Dock, now a pleasure marina by the Tower, alone accounted for the loss of 1,250 houses, displacing their inhabitants into neighbouring areas. The slums had come to London.

North and west London in the early 1800s showed the other side of the coin, reflecting the new prosperity in the spread of residential estates. Mansions and parkland yielded to their owners' realisation of the enhanced value that the needs of an expanding population was putting on their property. Perhaps the most significant of these developments centred on the Crown-owned lands of Marylebone Park. John Nash, the Prince Regent's architect, set out to create a garden city of villas and terrace houses for the rich in a Regent's Park connected by a triumphal way to the Prince's palace at Carlton House near Charing Cross. Compromise eventually reduced the promised 26 villas to eight and halved the circus to a single Park Crescent. Carlton House it-self was demolished in favour of Carlton House Terrace.

Horse Guards in formation

London on the Move

Improved communications had exercised the minds of the au-thorities for some time, and they focused on the river crossings. Waterloo, Southwark and Vaux-hall bridges joined the existing bridges, Westminster and Black-friars, at the beginning of the 19th century, and the medieval London Bridge was finally aban-doned in favour of a new bridge, higher upstream, begun in 1831.

The unit of wheeled power was still the horse, and Mr Shilli-beer's omnibus was bringing a new mobility to Londoners, but a horse of a different metal was about to change the face of Lon-don. In 1841 the London and Blackwall Railway brought the first commuters to the City's Fen-church Street. Most of the subse-quent termini were not allowed so close to the centre, but the last miles of iron road through built-up areas were responsible for the loss of thousands of houses and created extensive slum areas.

The train sheds of the rail stations drew architects to the use of glass and iron as evidenced in Bunning's pioneering Coal Exchange in Lower Thames Street. Paxton's palace of crystal for the Great International Exhibition of 1851 in Hyde Park was a natural step forward. His design, a doodle on a blotting pad, is as well known as a Leonardo cartoon. Here, the Victorians showed what Britain could make to over six million visitors, and took in over £400,000 at the turnstiles. Prince Albert, Queen Victoria's Consort, used the profits to build the Victoria and Albert Museum in the market gardens of South Kensington.

A fire that destroyed the old Palace of Westminster in 1834 provoked wholesale rebuilding on the site. The new Houses of Parliament might have looked very different, but of the two styles on offer to the competing architects, Elizabethan or Gothic, Charles Barry, with Pugin's help, won approval for his astonishing tour de force. Gothic was the flavour of the age. By 1847 the House of Lords was completed, followed by the Commons and Big Ben in 1858 and the Victoria Tower two years later.

Familiar landmarks and streetscapes were dropping into place. Victorian by-passes like the Embankment, Victoria Street and Chelsea Embankment liberated congested streets, and Holborn Viaduct ironed out the hills of Fleet valley. Shaftesbury Avenue and New Oxford Street cut swathes through the 'rookeries' of St Giles. 'Dwellings' began to appear as philanthropists like the American George Peabody tackled the shame of London's poor, and a new London County Council took on the problems of a city grown out of all proportion, problems which were to be compounded by the horrendous damage of war.

The interior of the Lloyd's Building

The Blitz left huge areas of the East End, most of its population evacuated to the countryside, in ruins. An opportunity for imaginative rebuilding was lost. Many of the faceless tower blocks and offices that were built in the 1950s and 1960s in the gaps created by the bombs are now themselves coming down. In their place, some new and innovative buildings are going up and, in the process, transforming London's skyline. Even the 'square mile' of the original City, hub of the nation's business community and regarded as somewhat conservative, is not immune to change – as anyone who has seen Richard Rogers's controversial new Lloyd's Building (see Walk 4: *Tower and City*) will readily agree.

HISTORY

AD

43 Romans found Londinium.

60 London set on fire and destroyed by Boadicea.

1065 Westminster Abbey consecrated by Edward the Confessor.

1066 William the Conqueror crowned in Westminster Abbey.

1097 Completion of the Tower of London's White Tower.

1190 London's first mayor.

1215 Magna Carta signed.

1265 First English Parliament.

1269 Present Westminster Abbey is consecrated.

1348 Beginning of the Black Death; 60,000 – half of London's population – die.

1476 Caxton's first printing press set up at Westminster.

1509 Henry VIII builds St James's Palace.

1536 Henry instigates the Dissolution of the Monasteries.

1558 Accession of Elizabeth I.

1585 William Shakespeare arrives in London.

1588 Final defeat of the Spanish Armada in the English Channel.

1598 Globe Theatre built.

1605 Guy Fawkes fails to blow up the Houses of Parliament.

1625 Inigo Jones completes the Banqueting House.

1631 Covent Garden laid out.

1635 Inigo Jones's Queen's House, Greenwich (now the Maritime Museum) is completed.

1649 Charles I executed at the Banqueting House.

1660 Restoration of the monarchy; Charles II becomes king.

1665 The Great Plague; a total of 100,000 people die.

1666 The Great Fire of London; half the city is destroyed.

1666–1723 Christopher Wren rebuilds St Paul's and 51 other London churches.

1806 Nelson buried in St Paul's.

1815 John Nash lays out Regent's Park, Regent Street and The Mall.

1824 National Gallery founded.

1829 First London police force and London bus (horse drawn).

1835 Building work begins on the Houses of Parliament.

1836 London's first passenger railway opens for business.

1837 Accession of Queen Victoria; Buckingham Palace becomes the Sovereign's official residence.

1843 Nelson's Column erected.

1847 British Museum completed.

1851 The Great Exhibition takes place in Hyde Park.

1863 London's first underground railway line opens.

1894 Tower Bridge is completed.

1905 Harrods' present shop opens.

1914–18 World War I.

1926 The General Strike.

1939–45 World War II; the Blitz destroys much of the City and the East End.

1951 Festival of Britain; the Festival Hall opens.

1952 Accession of Elizabeth II.

1956 Passing of the Clean Air Act brings an end to smog.

1965 Post Office Tower opens.

1973 New London Bridge.

1976 National Theatre opens.

1981 NatWest Tower completed, then, at 600ft, London's tallest building.

1986 Greater London Council abolished. The Lloyd's Building is completed.

1991 Canary Wharf, London's tallest building completed in the restored Docklands area.

London is a city that you can only really get to know by walking the streets. The first five walks in this guide show you the major sights that every visitor comes to see. The next seven walks, in the *Pick and Choose* section, are designed for visitors who have the time to explore London further, and they show you some of the author's favourite London districts. Lastly, the *Day Trips* section takes you by way of the Thames to the museums and royal palaces at Greenwich and Hampton Court.

Covent Garden and Soho

A day spent exploring the Covent Garden area, with its buskers, shops and quality restaurants, and seedy but chic Soho, home to London's Chinatown. The day ends at Leicester Square.

—Start at Tottenham Ct Road Stn, Northern and Central lines—

Walk away from the unmissable skyscaper Centre Point, and head down St Giles High Street for the serenity of **St Giles in the Fields** (9am–4pm). Henry Flitcroft's rebuilding of the church in the 1730s mirrors the work of Wren and Gibbs at St Martin-in-the-Fields, and the decoration of the interior in subtle tints of colour and gilt is most exquisitely done. Look for the **monument to George Chapman**, translator of Homer. It was designed by his friend Inigo Jones.

Imagine yourself manacled, in a cart, on your way to be hanged at Tyburn Tree. **The Angel**, the ordinary enough pub next to the church, is where you would have had your last pint. This was the last inn on the country lane that led to the gallows at Marble Arch.

Continue to the junction with Shaftesbury Avenue. Pedestrianised **Neal Street**, opposite you on the left, has all the flavour of Covent Garden's new image in its shops and craft workshops – Eastern instruments, natural shoes, baskets and kites, laced with restaurants biased to lentils and yoghurt. This is the London of the trendy, the young and the beautiful. First right in Shorts Gardens is the entrance to **Neal's Yard**, a cornucopia of grains, dried fruit, cereals and peanut butter, their heady aromas mixing with the smell of freshly baked bread. There's healthy eating here, as well as walk-in massage, aromatherapy – or any therapy you want. Look out for the fabulous cheese shop just beyond the Yard. Also on Shorts Gardens, notice the eccentric and entertaining water-driven sculpture that functions as a clock above the wholefood warehouse window. Behind you here is the entrance to a new shopping centre, **Thomas Neal's**, with exclusive but alternative shopping full of interesting ideas in an elegant glass-house setting. Continue down Neal Street to the end – passing **Neal Street East** on your right, a warehouse of Asian arts – then nip across Long Acre and into James Street,

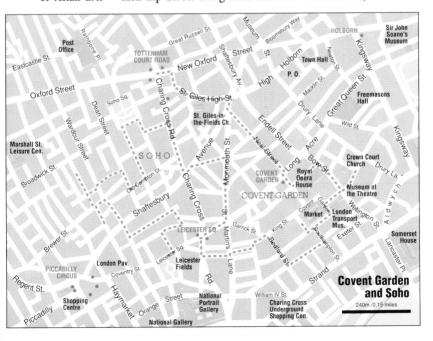

Covent Garden and Soho
240m /0.15 miles

The former covered market in Covent Garden

with the market just ahead. But first go left into Floral Street and right on Bow Street, home of the 'Bow Street Runners', the forerunners of the police. Opposite the police station is the **Royal Opera House**. The third on the site, it is an imposing building, though dull, with a richly decorated auditorium and good acoustics.

Russell Street leads left to the **Drury Lane Theatre**, like the Opera House vulnerable to fire and the fourth on this site since 1663. With many Georgian features, the ghost-haunted theatre has seen a procession of great names – Garrick, Sheridan, Kean, Sarah Siddons and Nell Gwynne, the local girl who sold oranges on opening nights, became an actress, and won a king's heart.

Don't feel you must dress up for the **Theatre Museum** (Tuesday–Sunday 11am–7pm, Café) in Russell Street. This beautifully mounted tribute to the performing arts gives you a seat in the stalls for a thousand performances of musical comedy and melodrama, circus and panto, all for the price of one seat in the gallery. Just round the corner is the **Transport Museum** (daily 10am–6pm). How did ladies preserve their modesty on the knifeboard omnibus?

The market fills **Covent Garden**, London's first square, originally the Convent Garden of Westminster Abbey. In the 1630s the fourth Earl of Bedford had the imagination to ask Inigo Jones to lay out a new residential estate. Houses in the terraces facing the square were set above arcades as in the Rue de Rivoli in Paris, but the only vestige of the 'Great Piazza' remaining is a re-created portion on the north side. The Duke later exploited the garden as a vegetable market, frightening off respectable tenants, and fathering the produce market which moved to Nine Elms in 1974.

In the centre is the **Apple Market** (weekdays 9am–6pm), given over to British craftspeople, and surrounding it are speciality shops like Pollock's, home of the toy theatre and the 'Penny Plain, Twopence Coloured' prints that have fascinated lovers of the theatre for generations. **The Punch & Judy** pub is a reminder that nearby Punch's Puppet Show was first performed in England. Samuel Pepys, the London diarist, was there.

Whatever the weather, you can enjoy eating outside here, thanks to the glass canopies, and enjoy the entertainment provided by the buskers. What finer backdrop could they have than the canopied front of **St Paul's church**? This is however the rear of 'the handsomest barn in England', Inigo Jones's neat compromise to conform with the layout of the square. The entrance is through an arched passage off King Street. The thespians have made St Paul's their Valhalla; Prima Ballerina Tamara Karsavina, Donald Wolfit, Charles Chaplin and Noel Coward are remembered on the walls, among others.

A flavour of Neal Street

Go down King Street and cross into the pedestrianised New Row. Turn left into Bedfordbury and enter Goodwin's Court, which has a tiny entrance just 20 yards from the corner. Walk down the alley past picturesque bow fronts. Cross St Martin's Lane to the **Salisbury,** for a drink at the marble-topped bar and the dazzle of cut glass, mirrors, Art Nouveau lights. For lunch try fish at **Sheekey's** in St Martin's Court or French at **Chez Solange**, round the corner in Cranbourn Street. For an after-lunch browse, try Cecil Court's bookshops, or take in the **Photographers' Gallery** (Tuesday–Saturday, 11am–7pm).

Continue up Monmouth Street to **Seven Dials** and the newly renewed obelisk. The original has been at Weybridge in Surrey since the 1730s. One of the seven sundials faces down Earlham Street, a microcosm of an earlier London, with street stalls, a butcher called

The Punch & Judy pub

Soho Square

Portwine, and Collins the ironmonger, in whose bosky interior can be found just about everything. At Cambridge Circus turn right up Charing Cross Road to **Foyle's**, once the world's largest bookshop, and Manette Street, which owes its name to Dickens's Dr Manette in *A Tale of Two Cities*, and is a fitting introduction to Soho, where French émigrés found refuge from the Revolution. Soho was once seedy London, but trendy bars and shops have moved in, catering for the media businesses here.

Turn right in Greek Street to **Soho Square**. Most of its 18th-century houses have been surrendered to commerce, but No 1 Greek Street has enjoyed a charmed life thanks to the **House of Charity**. Although only open at lunchtime, two days a week, the magnificent staircase and plasterwork can be glimpsed from the street. Charles II shares the square's garden with a ventilation shaft heavily disguised as a half-timbered cottage! At No 6 Frith Street, just south of the Square, William Hazlitt, the critic and essayist, breathed his last words, 'Well, I've had a happy life,' which should please visitors to Hazlitt's, the hotel. Celebrities stay here.

Old Compton Street runs a narrow gauntlet between restaurants, cafés, vintners and grocers, with French character in the Greek Street patisseries of **Valerie** and **Maison Bertaux**. Off Dean Street, where Karl Marx wrote *Das Kapital*, Meard Street leads to Peter Street and **Berwick Market**, London's best open-air market. Squeeze through Walker's Court, to the comparative calm of **Rupert Street**, with more stalls, choicer goods and higher prices. From Brewer Street turn right in Wardour Street, home to Britain's film industry. On the left is the tower of **St Anne**, Soho's parish church, with its incongruous 'beer barrel' spire.

Cross Shaftesbury Avenue on Wardour Street and turn left into

pedestrian Gerrard Street, better known as **Chinatown**, where the street signs are in Chinese as well as English, and the open gates make it a welcoming yet foreign place. New **Fook Lam Noon** wait on customers at No 10. Turn right at the end into Newport Place and right again into Lisle Street. Between here and Leicester Square is the French church, **Notre Dame de France**, and in the peace of its side chapel, a mural by Jean Cocteau. **Leicester Square**, with the Swiss Centre's performing clock, the city's major first-run cinemas and bustling crowds, is a popular meeting place. At night, when the clubs open, the square heaves with people.

The Swiss Centre

Walk (2)

Royal Progress

From Trafalgar Square to Whitehall, in time to see Changing of the Guard; past Henry VIII's wine cellars, through leafy St James's Park to the royal residences of the Queen Mother (St James's Palace) and the Queen (Buckingham Palace).

—*Start at Charing Cross Stn, Bakerloo, Jubilee, Northern lines*—

Thank heaven for the royals, for without them where would we the commoners be? So much of the history and character of London has been shaped by kings and queens, either by intent or default, that we owe them this tribute to the distinguished and beautiful buildings and the green and pleasant places that link them.

'If it's good enough for Nelson, it's quite good enough for me,' runs the old music hall song. **Trafalgar Square** has always been a people's place, the home of demonstrations and freedom of speech, yet its royal associations make it a good starting point. From the portico of the **National Gallery** (Monday–Saturday, 10am–6pm; Sunday, 2–6pm) you get a good view at bus-top level. Here was the Royal Mews when the Prince Regent, later George IV, had his residence at Carlton House nearby. The columns which frame Nelson, and, more distantly, St Stephen's Tower, were re-used when the Gallery was built in 1838. The gallery has recently been extended

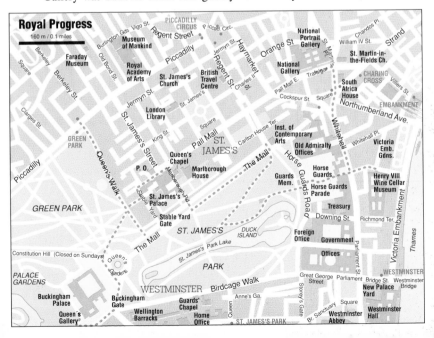

Nelson's Column

with the Sainsbury Wing, which earned recent royal approval from Prince Charles. Tucked away behind the National Gallery on Charing Cross Road is the **National Portrait Gallery** (Monday–Friday, 10am–6pm; Saturday, 10am–6pm; Sunday, 12–6pm), where the first requisite is a likeness, and artistic excellence merely accidental. They are not averse to mounting temporary exhibitions, even using photographs! Don't spend too long in either gallery if your priority is to catch Changing the Guard in Whitehall at 11am.

In Trafalgar Square's north-east corner George IV sits astride a horse, rather unhappily, since he has no saddle, boots or stirrups. James II by Grinling Gibbons, on the lawn in front of the National Gallery, fares little better. Hand on hip, he is inexplicably dressed as an ancient Roman!

When **St Martin-in-the-Fields**, which overlooks the square, was completed in 1726, one of the parishioners, who had already paid for nearly half the cost, gave the workmen a bonus of 100 guineas. That generous benefactor was none other than George III. The masterpiece of architect James Gibbs, St Martin's has the royal arms over the portico as well as over the chancel arch, and royalty sits in London's only royal pew. Charles II was baptised here, and his mistress, Nell Gwynne, was buried in the churchyard. Today the church has a good cafe and London's Brass Rubbing Centre.

Opposite South Africa House is the square's other column – a lamp standard that is a police station in disguise. Charles I cuts a

Changing the Guard

better figure on a horse in the fine equestrian statue by Hubert le Sueur that faces down Whitehall. Cast in 1633, the Civil War and consequent loss of the monarchy intervened before it could be erected, and it was sold for scrap to a Mr Rivett, a brazier. Once Charles II was back on the throne, the statue was miraculously resurrected and set on the plinth Sir Christopher Wren may have designed.

Whitehall, the street leading from Trafalgar Square, once connected the City of London with the great Abbey of Westminster. It cuts through the site of a royal palace that was the seat of power. Now it is lined with public buildings, and finishes at the Palace of Westminster, a people's palace and the seat of democratic government. On the right is the **Horse Guards**, where the Household Cavalry, the Sovereign's bodyguard on state occasions, mount a picturesque ceremony – Changing the Guard (Monday–Saturday, 11am; Sunday 10am). Cameras click, horses nod, commands are shouted, and the troop returns to their Knightsbridge Barracks. The courtyard is left to two guardsmen to stamp a path through the crowd.

The **Banqueting House** (Monday–Saturday, 10am–5pm; closed Sunday), facing the Horse Guards, is the only remaining building of Whitehall Palace. The Tudor buildings, where Henry VIII married Anne Boleyn, straddled the road behind the Holbein Gate. Following a fire, Inigo Jones was asked by James I to draw up plans for a new palace, but only the Banqueting House was built. Finished in 1622, it was probably London's first in Portland stone, and first in the style of Palladio. It must have looked astonishingly avant-garde rising from the huddle of timber-and-brick buildings. Inside, the Rubens ceiling provides a robust contrast in style to the architecture.

Relaxing in St James's Park

Henry VIII's **Wine Cellar** is still there, buried under the new Ministry building on Horseguard's Avenue, but not in its original position. It was moved to accommodate the foundations! The terrace and steps are still

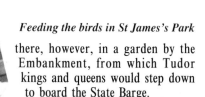
Feeding the birds in St James's Park

there, however, in a garden by the Embankment, from which Tudor kings and queens would step down to board the State Barge.

Cross back over to the Horse Guards and walk through the arch to **Horse Guards Parade**, where Trooping the Colour is performed on the Queen's official birthday. The best view is looking back across the parade ground at the Whitehall buildings. William Kent, the leading revivalist of Palladio, is usually credited with the design. To the north are the Admiralty and the Treasury, and to the south **Downing Street**, 'home' to the Prime Minister. Beyond are the **Cabinet War Rooms** (daily 10am–6pm), the underground labyrinth from which Churchill masterminded the strategy that finally released Londoners from the tyranny of the Luftwaffe.

Ahead is the inviting peace of **St James's Park**. Henry VIII drained a swamp for it. Charles II had it tricked out in the French taste with a straight canal, and let in the public to admire it. George IV's architect, John Nash, put a bend in the lake and gave it an island and a bridge with the best views in London. His landscaping is full of delightful incidents, disguising the fact that it is all on a very small scale. Visitors are entertained by a large variety of waterfowl, and you can have a ringside seat from the **Cake House** (10am–6.30pm), and perhaps scatter crumbs for the apparently insatiable birds. There are lunch alternatives in Storey's Gate, or in Victoria Street at that palace amongst pubs, the **Albert.**

Beyond the Mall, the wide processional way to Buckingham Palace, is Nash's **Carlton House Terrace**, divided by the Duke of York's Steps. The **Duke of York's Column**, on the site of the Prince Regent's mansion, was paid for by stopping a day's pay from all ranks of the army. Tucked under the Terrace is the ultimate cultural drop-in, the **Institute of Contemporary Arts** (Monday to Saturday, 12am–11pm; Sunday, 12am–10.30pm), gallery, cinema, café, bar, bookshop, or just talk, the freedom of it all on a Day Pass.

Next on the right are the garden walls of **Marlborough House**, built by Wren. It was the home of Queen Mary, grandmother of the present Queen, till her death in 1953. In Marlborough Gate is the **Queen's Chapel**, designed by Inigo Jones, and built before the road existed. The first church in England in the new, classical style, it was intended for the Infanta Maria of Spain, but completed for another Maria, Henrietta, whom Charles I married in 1625. The interior can be viewed by worshippers on Sunday mornings in summer.

St James's Palace is a very private place. Many royals were born in the Palace, and one, Charles I, walked from here to his death in Whitehall. Left past the Gatehouse and left again brings us to the **Stable Yard** with a modest range of buildings on the north side by Hawksmoor facing **Lancaster House**. The building once served as the London Museum, but has now been extravagantly refurbished for government entertaining. A passage leads to **Green Park** and Queen's Walk, named after George II's queen.

Buckingham Palace was never intended to be a palace, but had greatness thrust upon it, beginning life in 1715 as the Duke of Buckingham's country house. What you see is architect Sir Aston Webb's façade of 1913, but it is only skin-deep. What you don't see, because it faces the park, is John Nash's 1830s transformation for George IV. Strapped for cash to finish the job, Nash was replaced by Edward Blore, whose work was largely wallpapered over by Webb. A limited area of the palace (entrance in Buckingham Palace Road) opened to the public in 1993, and tickets were sold at a kiosk at the end of the Mall facing the palace.

Changing the Guard (11.30am daily in summer; every alternate day at other times of year) with the Queen in residence, and the royal standard flying, is an impressive and colourful ceremony that has the edge on the Horse Guards. It comes with music from the Guards' band, too. The dull mix of Buckingham Palace Road is redeemed by the imposing entrance to the **Royal Mews** (12–4pm one to three days a week according to season, closed during Ascot week). Here are the Queen's horses and coaches, including the Coronation Coach built for George III in 1762. The Queen shares her pictures with the public in the **Queen's Gallery** (Tuesday–Saturday, 10am–5pm; Sunday, 2am–5pm. Closed Monday). From here Victoria Station is just around the corner.

Buckingham Palace

West End

A tour of London's main shopping district from the fashion of Carnaby Street to the up-market tailors, wine merchants and antique dealers of St James's and Burlington Arcade. Art at the Royal Academy and ethnography at the Museum of Mankind.

—Start at Oxford Circus Stn, Bakerloo, Central, Victoria lines—

More than a geographical description of where the City leaves off, the name 'West End' confers on its inhabitants, workpeople and visitors alike, its accolade of breeding, affluence and fashion. That it most nearly identifies with the boundaries of Mayfair is no accident, or that the Duke of Westminster's Grosvenor Estate covers most of that, and that Grosvenor is one of our richest men. The aristocrats have left their grand houses, and in their place are high class hotels, restaurants, embassies and clubs. Above all, there are shops, popular in Oxford Street, moving up-market through Regent Street to the refinement of Piccadilly and Bond Street. Shops, then, are the main attraction, but museums and art galleries flourish too in the rich soil of the West End.

The first turning down Regent Street, Little Argyll Street, leads to the **London Palladium**, the Music Hall that followed a circus,

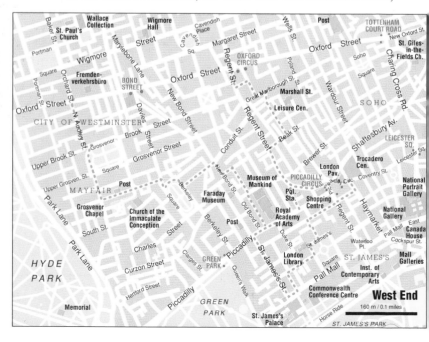

where anything could happen on stage from *The Pirates of Penzance* to the Ram Jam Band, and probably will. In Great Marlborough Street you may be forgiven for thinking Mr Liberty a little backward-looking, but building his store **Liberty** in 'Tudor' style in 1924 showed him to be an astute businessman. The timbers are genuine enough; they came from England's wooden battleships. On the bridge that connects with the Regent Street building, St George rings bells and never quite succeeds in catching an elusive dragon every 15 minutes.

Liberty turns the corner into **Carnaby Street**. Time was when swinging London swung highest here. It still has its attractions but, despite refurbishment, it is a little threadbare, as Shakespeare might have said, 'by Time's fell hand defaced'. He looks down on the crowds from a niche high on the corner of the **Shakespeare's Head**, though the pub's connection is not with William, but with Thomas and John Shakespeare, who owned the inn in 1735. The pervading smell is of leather, usually black and studded with shiny metal decoration. The noise is the amplified thud of rock music. Even Inderwick's, pipe specialists for generations, and the only surviving shop from the days before the street gained its current reputation, has hubblebubble pipes in its windows instead of meerschaums.

Turn right in Beak Street and continue down Regent Street past **Garrard**, the Crown Jeweller, though they do sell to commoners, and drop into the **Café Royal**. It is still possible to discover in the plush and gilt interior something

The clock outside Liberty

of the attraction the place had for Oscar Wilde, Aubrey Beardsley, Augustus John and other literary and artistic people, but the price of one drink will no longer buy you an evening's entertainment.

Just across Regent Street is **Veeraswamy's Restaurant** (entrance at Victory House, 99–101 Swallow Street) which recalls the days of the British Raj. At Piccadilly Circus, in Glasshouse Street, and framed in the arches of the County Fire Office, is the first of London's Chinese restaurants, the **Cathay**, with a sidelong view of London's 'Big Top'. There are many sideshows here – **The London**

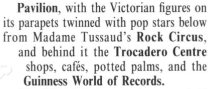

Pavilion, with the Victorian figures on its parapets twinned with pop stars below from Madame Tussaud's **Rock Circus**, and behind it the **Trocadero Centre** shops, cafés, potted palms, and the **Guinness World of Records.**

The life of the streets is more vivid and interesting. Cross the Circus to Lower Regent Street, and taste tea as it should be brewed, in the **Ceylon Tea Centre** in Jermyn Street. The latter is shopping street by appointment to clubland and St James's. Windows offer with great discretion ties, shirts, shoes, perfume and jewellery, but what are **Paxton & Whitfield** doing at No 93? The answer is in the cheese and the choice. 'Cottenham on the straw, Sir? Certainly, Sir.' Across the road, and snugly tucked into the entrance to St James's Piccadilly, is the wholefood café, **Wren at St James's**. A step or two and we are in Wren's new church for a growing suburb. Badly damaged in World War II and recreated, it has a reredos of carved fruit and flowers and a carved marble 'garden of Eden' font by Grinling Gibbons. More Gibbons in the angels that trumpet above the magnificent organ from the chapel of Whitehall Palace.

The **Red Lion** in Duke of York Street is deceptive. This tiny pub seems so much bigger inside. The secret is in the cut glass mirrors that surround the walls and produce endless reflections of their beautiful decoration, all set in the dark mahogany frame of the bar furniture. Down the hill is **St James's Square**, laid out in 1660, with imposing houses of the 18th century that have seen the birth of a king, George III, and been the residence of the dukes of Norfolk, the bishops of London, and at No 10, Chatham House, of three prime ministers. This quiet backwater has been touched violently by modern events. General Eisenhower planned the inva-

Piccadilly Circus

Burlington Arcade

sion of Africa and France here at No 31, and during a demonstration outside the Libyan People's Bureau in 1984 WPC Yvonne Fletcher was shot dead. She is remembered in a memorial by the railing of the gardens.

Walk clockwise round the Square's equestrian William III to King Street. Opposite **Christie's**, the famous auction rooms, is Crown Passage and the **Golden Lion**, a drinking house with the second oldest licence in the West End, and a tiny bar which confers a quick intimacy on its customers. Turn right in Pall Mall to St James's Street and the remarkable survival of clubland's Georgian shopping parade. If you are a privileged customer at **Berry Bros and Rudd**, the wine merchants, they will record your weight on their giant scales, just as they did that of the Prince Regent, who might well have patronised **Lock's**, next door. Established in 1759, London's 'top' hatters have an interesting display in their windows. Between the shops is the narrow passage leading to **Pickering Place**, a Georgian backwater it is difficult to associate with gambling and bloodshed, but it is credited with having been the scene of London's last duel.

Clubs, carefully guarding their anonymity, line the street. **Boodles** is perhaps everything it should be, with an imposing Adam-style front, and a huge Venetian window which lights a very private world. Turn right in Piccadilly and hope to catch the action on the hour of **Fortnum and Mason**'s clock. Their food hall is where the Queen shops for her groceries. Enjoy the lively view from the restaurant before investigating Piccadilly's arcades.

On the north side is **Burlington House** (daily 10am–6pm), the home of the Royal Academy of Arts, and, if it is summer, host to works submitted by living artists. Buy now, but don't hope to collect till mid-August. At other times the Academy mounts exhibitions as fund-raising support to help maintain its art school. The building itself entombs part of the Earl of Burlington's town house built in the 1660s, and occasional access can be had to a fine suite of rooms. The rest is ponderous Victorian.

The **Burlington Arcade**, next door, is frivolous by comparison, but that does not mean that you can whistle

Cork Street art gallery

or, for that matter, hurry through this promenade of Regency shops. The Beadles will get you if you do. Turn right in Burlington Gardens for the **Museum of Mankind** (Monday–Saturday, 10am–5pm; Sunday 2.30–6pm), where the ethnography department of the British Museum has taken refuge. Exciting temporary exhibitions are presented against a background of permanent displays.

You may find echoes of tribal art across the road in **Cork Street**, which is almost wall-to-wall gallery, and all of it free. All shades of art appreciation are catered for, and feelings outraged at the Piccadilly Gallery can be soothed at Browse and Darby or the Redfern next door. Turn left in Clifford Street and from the right-hand side of New Bond Street look down to the **Time & Life Building**. Above the low-level link is a frieze by Henry Moore.

It is difficult to believe that **Bruton Street** was in such recent residential occupation that there could have been a royal birth there in the 1920s, but there is a plaque to prove it on the wall of Berkeley Square House – 'Queen Elizabeth, born April 21, 1926'. **Berkeley Square** itself has only lately succumbed to the gambling casinos and advertising agencies. The chinoiserie **Pump House** in the centre is still there, but the nightingale has flown. On the west side a few good 18th-century houses linger on. **Mount Street**, which runs off the top left-hand corner of the square, is a confection in pink terracotta iced with the **Connaught**, the hotel with the enviable reputation, Scott's seafood restaurant, and the Audley, the pub with the 'English Dining Room'.

Under the watchful eye of the eagle above the US Embassy (heavily guarded, as you will soon discover if you loiter), South Audley Street engages Grosvenor Square, and leaves as North Audley Street for Oxford Street. Head this way if you feel the urge for more shopping. **Selfridges** anybody?

Selfridges In Oxford Street

WALK 4

Tower and City

Two faces of the city of London; archaeological remains as old as the city itself and the brand-new Design Museum; see the Crown Jewels, the restored Docklands and revered restaurants where gents still down their oysters with champagne.

—Start at Tower Hill Station, District and Circle lines—

From the beginning the Tower and the City were the power and the glory of England's capital by the Thames, exercising military and monetary control often with a crushing disregard for human life. For nearly 400 years traitors imprisoned in the Tower were brought to Tower Hill above the river for the public spectacle of their execution, the exact spot recorded by a stone pavement in **Trinity Square Garden**. Heads rolled but others were saved. Nearby, in the elegant, 18th-century Trinity House, the Trinity Brethren were building lighthouses and providing pilots for greater safety at sea. Beside them on the hill are several stretches of the City's **Roman wall**.

Turn your back on the monstrous former headquarters of the Port of London Authority topped by the statue of Neptune, and look riverwards to the **Tower of London** (March–October: Monday–Saturday, 9am–5pm; Sunday, 10am–5pm; November–February: Monday–Saturday, 9am–4pm; Sunday 10am–4pm. Last

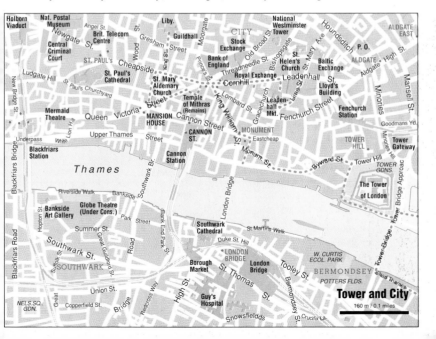

Tower and City

160 m / 0.1 miles

The Tower of London

guided tour 2.30pm), which surely inspires every child's toy fort, but is unequalled as a work of great military architecture. William the Conqueror's White Tower, England's only complete Norman keep, dominates the surrounding walls and bastions, its corner turrets renewed, like capped teeth, in the 14th century. Inside is the **Chapel of St John**, looking as if it had been hollowed from solid rock, immensely impressive in its strength and simplicity. As an antidote take in the **Crown Jewels** and see what Charles II wore on formal occasions, or hear from a picturesquely garbed Beefeater just why ravens are on the payroll (legend says that if they ever leave, the Tower will crumble). A line of washing on the battlements comes as no surprise; there is still a garrison here. **Gun Wharf** along the river gives a different view of **Traitors' Gate** from that enjoyed by the wretches landed here by boat.

It is difficult to take **Tower Bridge** (April–October: 10am–6.30pm; November–March: 10am–4.30pm) seriously, though it is the perfect accompaniment to the Tower, and conceals the engineering expertise of the Victorians (it was built in 1894) in raising by steam the great bascules of the road bridge. The high-level walkway gives a great view of *HMS Belfast*. If you are feeling energetic, then cross the bridge briefly to Butler's Wharf, Hays Galleria (with its amazing water-powered sculpture) and the Conran Foundation **Design Museum** (Tuesday–Sunday, 11.30am–6.30pm; closed Monday). Meet old and familiar friends here – everyday things like a bicycle or a chair – and learn why they look like they do, or did.

The Tower Thistle Hotel introduces **St Katharine's Dock**, which has taken on a new life as London's marina. Telford's fine warehouses, once piled with ivory tusks, are the backdrop for Thames

Tower Bridge

A Beefeater at the Tower of London

barges. Enjoy the nautical ambience at the **Dickens Inn**, and come back for the medieval banquet in the Beefeater Restaurant.

Lower Thames Street runs drably from the Tower, past the Custom House (cross to the right side) to **St Magnus the Martyr**. Wren's richly furnished interior survives – pulpit and tester, gallery, organ of 1712, and altar paintings of high quality. The old London Bridge was originally much lower down than the present one, here overhead. Up Fish Street Hill stands the **Monument** (31 March–30 September: Monday –Friday, 9am–6pm; Saturday, Sunday, 2–6pm; 1 October–30 March: Monday–Saturday, 9am–4pm; closed Sunday), erected in 1671–7 by Wren to commemorate the Great Fire. In the relief on the pedestal Charles II cheers on the rebuilding of the devastated City, dressed improbably as a Roman. Catholics will be glad to learn that they are no longer blamed for the catastrophe, the original inscription having been changed. Not for the faint-hearted is the 202ft (61.5m) climb up the spiral stair for spectacular views.

From here take King William Street, a spoke in the wheel that revolves round the hub of financial London, **Bank**, **Royal Exchange**, and the Lord Mayor's residence, the **Mansion House**. In such company a lesser building than the parish church of St Mary Woolnoth at the corner of Lombard Street would be outfaced, but Hawksmoor's twin towers more than hold their own, even though tube station entrances burrow beneath. If your surname is Woolnoth you will discover its origin inside; it was the name given to illegitimate children when they were baptised. Tucked behind the columned and pedimented front of the Mansion House is another Wren creation, **St Stephen Walbrook**, on Walbrook, which is poised above

Mansion House

another hidden stream. Walk up the steps and you are climbing Walbrook's bank. With St Stephen, Wren was obviously feeling his way towards St Paul's dome and lantern over a central space. Now the eye goes to Henry Moore's massive altar table, pagan

almost in its primitive simplicity. In contrast a glorious organ looks down on the circling, contemporary seats.

Turn left in Queen Victoria Street for Temple Court, and in its forecourt the remains of the excavated **Temple of Mithras**, brought from the site of Bucklersbury House nearby, and strangely elevated and isolated among forbidding office blocks. **Sweetings**, the fish restaurant on the corner of Queen Street, looks older and has all the earmarks of a City institution – marble slabs, white linen, and City men on stools and in a hurry downing their oysters. Cross, right, to Bow Lane for an office worker's cuppa in the Bow Snack Bar, and so to Cheapside's **St Mary-le-Bow**. Wren's masons built well. The magnificent tower and steeple escaped the fires of the Blitz that destroyed the bells. Gutted and restored, the body of the church has little charm and, mystifyingly, two pulpits.

Turn right down Cheapside and left in King Street. Beyond its yard is the **Guildhall** (daily 10am–5pm, closed Sunday in winter). There is little medieval about it now, except for its outline, but fires, bombing and modern additions fail to diminish its status as one of London's most important civic buildings. Guests at the frequent banquets share the Great Hall with Nelson and Wellington, a leaden Churchill and, above the gallery, the gilded figures of Gog and Magog, the City's giants. Sir Nicholas Throckmorton was not so lucky. An inscription records that at his trial in the hall for high treason, the jury's verdict of not guilty was deemed unsatisfactory, and they were sent to prison themselves until they came up with a more acceptable result.

At the rear of Guildhall to the left is the **Guildhall Library** (Monday–Saturday, 9.30am–5pm), where one of the City guilds, the Worshipful Company of Clockmakers, puts on a permanent exhibition of their considerable contribution to horology (not open Saturday). Even more fascinating is the **Museum of London**, reached by continuing up Gre-

sham Street and turning right up to the busy roundabout where the museum sits. Inside you will find all the best archaeological finds discovered in the City over the last four decades, plus the Lord Mayor's glittering coach (Tuesday–Saturday, 10am–6pm, Sunday 12–6pm). From the museum head south along St Martin's Le Grand, turn left along Cheapside and Poultry and then cross the Bank intersection into Cornhill. If the spirit of the old City exists anywhere it is here in the maze of little courts and alleys between Cornhill and Lombard Street. On the right is a good introduction, statues and fountains in a pedestrian square, but **Ball Court** (on the right, follow a sign to Simpson's) plunges you into the world of Thackeray and Dickens, with surprises at every turn. Here is **Simpson's** (open since 1759) with inviting offerings of steak and kidney pie and steamed puddings. A taste of the 18th century? Hard by at the **George and Vulture** Mr Pickwick is in the chair of the Pickwick Club, and in St Michael's Alley, history tells us that **Pasqua Rosée** served London's first cup of coffee in 1652. Above a tiny space where parishioners were buried, Hawksmoor's tower of **St Michael Cornhill** thrusts upwards to the light. Below, the **Jamaica Wine House** revels in the dark.

Just short of Gracechurch Street is a view of Wren's **St Peter upon Cornhill**, slotted between shops and offices, and smug in its claim to have beaten Canterbury as the earliest consecrated ground in England. Thackeray, in the editorial chair of the *Cornhill Magazine*, could see the church from his

The NatWest Tower

office window, and Charlotte Brontë arriving at her publishers, Smith and Elder. Pause at the Gracechurch Street corner and look left for one of those visual surprises that make the City's architectural excesses tolerable. At the foot of the shining black stump of the **NatWest Tower** is the white, wedding-cake extravagance of the former National Provincial Bank, dock leaf to NatWest's nettle. Cross to Leadenhall Street, and, first right on Whittington Avenue, **Leadenhall Market**, a fine covered arcarde. You bought your chicken here in the 14th

Lloyd's of London

century, and you can still buy one here, though the market is no longer solely devoted to poultry and meat. Christmases past, when it was festooned with turkeys to the heights of its Victorian glass-and-iron roof, are in the fading memories of older Londoners. The site of the market was the centre of Roman London, and below it was a basilica nearly as long as St Paul's Cathedral.

Lime Street, where the shipping lines come ashore, curves round the market to embrace **Lloyd's** (sadly closed to the public for the moment), where insurance underwriting, once conducted under Adam ceilings in a 1920s building, now operates from a glass-and-satin-steel complex. Watching the crawler lifts slide smoothly up and down the outside is a local pastime. For a real frisson, look through Sir Edwin Cooper's preserved entrance in Leadenhall Street at Richard Rogers's interior. The No 25 bus stop is opposite.

Walk 5

War and Peace

Relive the Blitz at the Imperial War Museum, then visit the Houses of Parliament and Westminster Abbey. Watch Parliament in session, or go to see the best of Turner's painting and modern art at the Tate Gallery. If you don't feel like too much walking, start this itinerary at Dean's Yard.

—Start at Lambeth North Station, Bakerloo Line—

This walk begins where the futility of war is recorded, in the old Bethlem Royal Hospital for the Insane. As a home for the **Imperial War Museum**, (daily 10am–6pm), 'Bedlam', as the hospital was popularly called, was an inspired choice. At the core is a series of displays called 'The Blitz Experience' which brings home just what Londoners went through during World War II.

What is not generally appreciated is the importance of the museum's collection of work by official war artists, often big names. It includes the series of paintings of Clyde shipbuilding by Stanley Spencer, outstanding works by Paul Nash, Graham Sutherland, Eric Ravilious, and moving images from World War I by Nevinson.

About a half mile down the rather bleak Lambeth Road are the

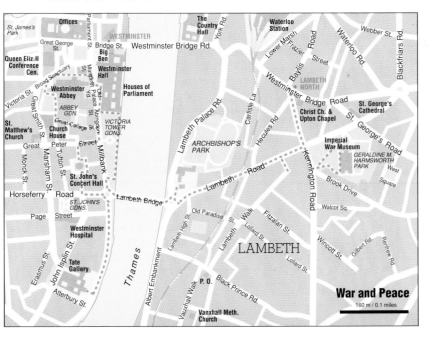

War and Peace

160 m / 0.1 miles

Palace of the Archbishops of Canterbury, and the parish church of St Mary's, born again as the **Museum of Garden History** (Monday–Friday, 11am–3pm; Sunday 10.30am–5pm; free). With no parishioners it needed friends, and the Tradescant Trust, gardeners all, not only rescued the church from decay, but created a museum and a garden. The Tradescants, who lived locally, were gardeners to Lord Salisbury and Charles I. The replica 17th-century garden, reached through the church, is planted with flowers and shrubs the Tradescants brought from abroad. John Tradescant died in 1638, and is buried here. Nearby lies Captain Bligh of the *Bounty*. He was also a plant hunter, and it was on an expedition to Tahiti to collect bread-fruit that the famous mutiny broke out.

Lambeth Palace, London home of the Archbishops of Canterbury for over 700 years, was on the river by the ferry steps until bridge and embankment put it across the road, but the group of buildings by St Mary's still makes an attractive composition. The twin-towered and red brick gatehouse, known as **Morton's Tower**, was built in 1495, and behind it is a 17th-century hall. Unfortunately access is limited to guided tours on Wednesday and Thursday, booked long in advance. Call the social secretary on 071 928 8282.

Lambeth says it with pineapples. The fruits topping the pillars at the bridge approach are a 'Thank you' to John Tradescant, the man who first brought them to England. Across the road from the palace is a riverside promenade with a good view of Parliament; television interviews with politicians are sometimes conducted here.

Cross Lambeth bridge towards the grand civil service and defence buildings and descend the steps on the right to the Victoria Tower Gardens. At the far end near the **Houses of Parliament** is a sombre group: the *Burghers of Calais*, Rodin's expression in bronze of compassion for the fate of the hostages to Edward III.

Great College Street opens opposite. Here, on the right, is the abbey's moat wall. Below our feet ran one of Tyburn's streams, which isolated Thorney Island on which Westminster Abbey stood. Through a gate in the wall is the **Abbey Garden** (Thursday 10am–6pm), used by the monks for the growing of herbs, and there is evidence that it was laid it out on a bed of oyster shells for drainage.

At the turn in the street is the entry to the very imposing and old **Dean's Yard**,

Museum of Garden History

Westminster Abbey

and on the right the restored monastic buildings of **Westminster School**, which had its origins in the abbey itself and provides the singers for the Abbey choir. Leave Dean's Yard through the arch of the Victorian office block, and the west front entrance to **Westminster Abbey** (donation) is on your right. What is so remarkable about this recently-cleaned cathedral-like building in the heart of London is that it is not in ruins, which it probably would be had it not been the crowning and burial place of kings and queens, the seat of government even. This special dispensation did not protect it from the restorers however, and, looking at the west towers, its most prominent aspect, there is little hint of the great Norman French abbey behind. What we see is English, and 18th-century English at that. Wren proposed and Hawksmoor disposed.

Go through the west door into the nave, where Henry Yevele's work in the 14th century blends into Henry de Reyn's of a century earlier. Its astounding proportions lift the eyes to the roof, the highest in England, and draw them down its great length. **Henry VII's Chapel**, not completed till 1519, is the most exciting part of the abbey with its spectacular fan-vaulted roof and huge windows made possible by the flying buttresses. Henry was to be remembered long after the 10,000 masses for his soul had been said. Over the

Henry VII's Chapel

stalls hang the banners and crests of the Knights of the Bath, but to see what life in the Middle Ages was like you should lift up the seats. Wives beat husbands in those days!

If you would like a 25 per cent discount off brass rubbing, then Guided Super Tours may be the answer to seeing the rest of the abbey's treasures, but they do take away the thrill of discovery. Scots may wish to avoid the Coronation Chair. It was made for Edward I, and designed to hold the ancient Stone of Scone, stolen from them in 1296.

Next to the Chapel of the Pyx in the Norman undercroft is the **Museum**, a mini-Tussaud's of lifelike effigies made for funeral pro-

cessions. Here are Henry VII – compare it with Torrigiani's sculptured head in the Chapel – Elizabeth I, Charles II, and Nelson.

Poets' Corner has to be the biggest draw. It began with Chaucer, buried here in 1400, but got out of hand in the 18th century, when it began to resemble the sculpture room at the Royal Academy. In the Cloisters, you come closest to the abbey's origin as a Benedictine monastery. In the north walk the monks worked on manuscripts, taking their meals in the Refectory by the south walk. In the east walk they were laid to rest. Nearby is the **Chapter House**, where the Great Council met in 1257. From Edward I to Henry VIII, it was used as Parliament House for the Commons. To this day the Dean and Chapter have no authority here.

Back outside, bear right round the abbey for **St Margaret Westminster**, which is the traditional parliamentary place of worship. Cross the street to the Houses of Parliament. One building stands out against the Victorian Gothic, the medieval **Westminster Hall**, sole survivor of the Palace of Westminster after the fire of 1834. Rebuilt in 1349 by Henry Yevele, it has been described as 'the finest timber-roofed building in Europe'. For hundreds of years it served as the law courts, and death was dispensed here to kings, bishops, earls and conspirators, including Guy Fawkes. We could have had an Elizabethan-style Parliament House, but the taste for Gothic prevailed and by 1860 the two Houses, designed by Barry with Pugin as his assistant, was completed. Barry was knighted; Pugin went insane. The **Strangers' Gallery** (2.30–10pm), entrance next to the Victoria Tower, allows viewing when the House is in session.

In Millbank turn right into Great Peter Street and left into

...and Rodin's 'Kiss'

Lord North Street, where bells ring in the Georgian houses to summon MPs to vote on divisions in the House. At the end is the silhouette of **St John, Smith Square**. Condemned as 'Queen Anne's Footstool', Thomas Archer's idiosyncratic church was burned out during the last war and became a concert hall. Regain Millbank via Horseferry Road and continue to the **Tate Gallery** (Monday–Saturday 10am–5.30pm, Sunday 2–5.30pm), greatly improved since Turner came to the **Clore Gallery**, and a more coherent hanging policy was adopted. The Victoria Line's Pimlico station is across Vauxhall Bridge Road.

1. Chelsea

Afternoon visit to London's oldest garden and the homes of many famous writers, with a glimpse of sunset on the Thames.

—Start at Sloane Square Station, Circle and District lines. Bus from Piccadilly—

There is more to Chelsea than just the famous King's Road. A few steps away from the boutiques, antique arcades and burger bars is the riverside village that Whistler loved to paint. Not that King's

Sloane Square's controversial theatre

Road doesn't have a good start. See how wonderfully the designers of **Peter Jones**, the department store, managed the transition from square to street in a deliciously sensuous curve.

At the other end of Sloane Square is the **Royal Court**, a theatre with a talent for experiment. Lower Sloane Street leads off the south side to Royal Hospital Road and, just past the Old Burial Ground, the main gate of Chelsea's **Royal Hospital** (Monday–Saturday, 10am–noon, 2–4pm; Sunday 2–4pm). Charles II took a leaf out of Louis XIV's book in providing a home for his old and disabled soldiers, and modelled it on the Hotel des Invalides in Paris. Some believe

Nell Gwynne added her persuasive powers. Sir Christopher Wren was appointed architect, and what could have been a forbidding institution was handled with great sympathy. The **Chapel,** consecrated

in 1691, has a splendid *Resurrection* painted by Sebastiano Ricci, and the **Great Hall,** where the Chelsea pensioners, who wear distinctive red uniforms, eat in style under the gaze of Verrio's *Charles II* on horseback, are most rewarding. The **Museum** has several surprising objects, such as tortoiseshell ear trumpets.

At the eastern end of the Hospital grounds is a garden on the site of one of London's famous 18th-century pleasure grounds – Ranelagh. Leave the path through the Hospital at the west end in Infirmary Road, and regain Royal Hospital Road past the stables. Turn left into Tite Street. No 34 was Oscar Wilde's 'House Beautiful', from which he edited *Woman's World*.

The entrance to **Chelsea Physic Garden** (April to October; Sunday, 2–6pm, Wednesday, Bank Holidays 2–5pm. Tel: 071-352 5646) is in Swan Walk. Founded by the Society of Apothecaries in 1673, it is second only to Oxford as the oldest botanic garden in the country, with thousands of rare and unusual plants including the largest olive tree outdoors in Britain, and – tea!

Where Chelsea Embankment meets Royal Hospital Road are two of the most important houses of the 1870s, **Cheyne House** and the

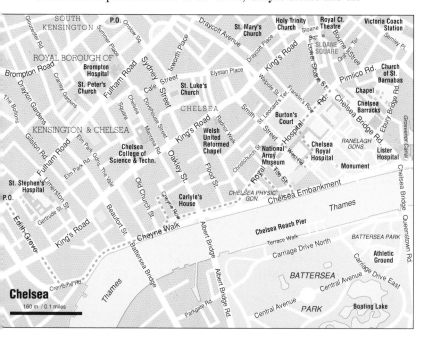

Chelsea

160 m / 0.1 miles

highly original **Swan House**, both by Norman Shaw. Cheyne Walk crosses Oakley Street and continues past the houses of the rich and influential, where even the street parking is for 'Diplomats' Cars Only'. Gardens and a road now separate it from the river, which was lined with the cottages and wharves of Chelsea village. Turn right into Cheyne Row, which has a good pub in the King's Head and Eight Bells, and find that time stands still in **Carlyle House** (April–end October, Wednesday–Sunday, Bank Holiday Mondays 11am–5pm). The Scottish historian, Thomas Carlyle, brought his wife Jane here to live in 1834 in a house built in the early 1700s. They left it wholly Victorian, papering over the panelling to modernise it, and it remains with its books, furniture and pictures, just as they left them. What the 'Sage of Chelsea' did not find was peace and quiet. His sound-proof attic study, built on the roof, failed to keep out the noise of cocks crowing, street musicians and horses' hooves. How would he have reacted to being in today's flightpath?

At the end of Cheyne Row turn left into Upper Cheyne Row and **Lawrence Street**, home of the Chelsea porcelain works from 1745–84. Dr Johnson fancied his hand at the wheel, but his pots never survived the firing! Halfway down Lawrence Street is a fascinating byway, **Justice Walk**, but continue on to Cheyne Walk and to confrontation with a lumpen, gilded Sir Thomas More, Chelsea's most important resident. Henry VIII's Chancellor went to the Tower, and was beheaded in 1535, having prepared his resting place in **Chelsea Old Church**. The church was nearly destroyed by a land mine in 1941 but, like the

The colour of King's Road

Portland vase, was lovingly reassembled from the shattered fragments and looks, you could say, as good as old. Amongst many distinguished monuments to distinguished people are two carved capitals by Holbein. Further west, across Church Street, is **Crosby Hall** (Monday–Friday, 10am–1pm, 2–5pm; Saturday–Sunday, 2–5pm), Chelsea's oldest house, yet only here since 1910. It was originally in Bishopsgate, the great hall of a wool merchant's mansion built between 1466 and 1475. The view upriver from the west end of **Cheyne Walk** can, given a sunset, still be a romantic one, and it must be the reason so many of the famous in art and literature came to live here – Whistler and Brunel in Lindsey House, Hilaire Belloc, Walter Greaves, Wilson Steer and Turner.

Suddenly the road turns away from the river at **Cremorne**, a sad scrap of garden where once Victorians danced the night away beneath the coloured lanterns. Edith Grove on the right will take you back to the buses of the King's Road.

2. Belgravia, Knightsbridge and South Kensington

Start at lunch-time with a choice of interesting pubs serving food, then on to Harrods and, if you have the energy, a choice of four splendid museums, including the V&A and the Natural History Museum.

—Piccadilly Line to Hyde Park Corner. Bus from Piccadilly—

A roundabout too big, but not big enough for so much traffic makes **Hyde Park Corner** a dangerous place to stand and stare. So slip away down Knightsbridge, and take the unpromising alley on the left into **Old Barrack Yard**. The Duke of Wellington paraded his men here before Waterloo, and stabled his horse through the archway on the right in the mews. His mounting block can still be seen outside **The Grenadier** public house.

Turn left in Wilton Crescent Mews and right in Wilton Crescent

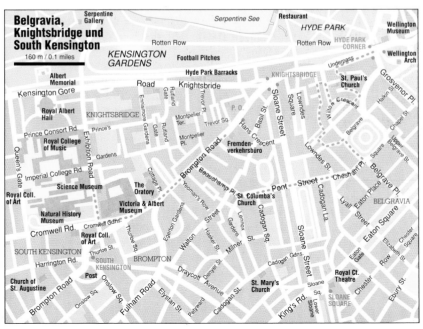

Harrods, Knightsbridge

to Wilton Place. Opposite St Paul's, where Society makes its vows, is the narrow entrance to Kinnerton Street, once the village street for coachmen and grooms, butlers and manservants. Thinly disguised, the coach houses and haylofts are there still, and so are the pubs. The tiny **Nag's Head** is known as 'the £11 pub'. That was what it was bought for in 1923! Motcomb Street vies with Bond Street as the artists' shop window. Catch the flavour of the 1990s at Michael Parkin's **Sickerts**. Most of the galleries in these streets welcome casual visitors, although you may well have to ring a bell on the door before being admitted.

Opposite, an inviting arcade leads to West Halkin Street. Cross left and turn the corner to the arched entrance of Belgrave Mews West, the service road to Belgrave Square's mansions. **The Star** is just about everything a public house should be, quiet and welcoming.

Back under the mews arch, turn right into **Belgrave Square**, so large the other side is out of sight. The square is the location of many foreign embassies. The sheer scale of its façades makes it a difficult place to come to terms with, and it is a relief to leave its south-west corner for Pont Street. Continue through Cadogan Square, but shed a sympathetic tear for Oscar Wilde, sitting in Room 53 of the **Cadogan Hotel**, getting quietly drunk on hock and seltzer, and waiting to be arrested.

Pont Street finishes beyond Sloane Street. Walton Street, which crosses here, might justify a gourmet's diversion, and **Beauchamp Place** mixes shops, restaurants and boutiques to make a very colourful street scene. A few yards right in the Brompton Road was a small grocer's shop lit, in 1848, by paraffin lamps. Today, **Harrods** is the largest store in Europe. The **Food Hall** defies superlatives, the art deco gentlemen's hairdresser is a delight, and so, I am told, is the ladies' lavatory.

To the left on the other side of Brompton Road is the **Victoria and Albert Museum** (Monday–Saturday, 10am–6pm; Sunday 2.30–6pm), built after the Great Exhibition of 1851 held in Hyde Park. The Victorians were rude about it, but the iron-and-glass construction survived to roof the East End's Museum of Childhood. The V&A, one of a clutch of museums centred on Exhibition Road, was completed by 1909, and contains a collection of decorative arts too large to detail. Across Exhibition Road is the **Natural History Museum** (Monday–Saturday, 10am–6pm; Sunday 2.30–6pm). In a curious way the Romanesque extravagance of the Victorian building suits the stuffed elephants and dinosaur skeletons.

Also in Exhibition Road is the **Science Museum** (Monday–Saturday, 10am–6pm; Sunday 11am–6pm), and the press-button joy of working models. Your opportunity to go down a mine makes the **Geological Museum** (Monday–Saturday, 10am–6pm; Sunday 2.30–6pm; an integral part of the Natural History Museum) more exciting than you might expect. Necessary refreshments are available in them all.

South Kensington Station, with the Piccadilly and District lines, is a few yards across Cromwell Road, and buses stop outside the Victoria and Albert Museum heading for Piccadilly.

3. Hyde Park

A leisurely morning or afternoon stroll through Hyde Park starting at the 'last' house in London, taking in the Serpentine Gallery and the State Apartments at Kensington Palace.

—Start at Hyde Park Corner Station, Piccadilly Line—

On May Day 1660, Pepys wrote in his diary: 'It being a very pleasant day I wished myself in Hyde Park.' The fact that 300 years later people still have the same idea says much for the enduring attraction of a place in the heart of a changed London.

Hyde Park Corner

For the Duke of Wellington it was his back garden. At **Apsley House** (Tuesday–Sunday 11am–5pm; closed Monday) the last (or first) house in Piccadilly, No 1 London as it was known, the victor of Waterloo made his home from 1817 to his death in 1852. His architects garnished Robert Adam's brick-built mansion with stone, columns and a portico, but much of the old Adam survives inside in the staircase, drawing room and portico room. Gratitude was heaped on the Duke in the form of plate and porcelain, paintings, some the spoils of war, sculpture and chandeliers. One gift, 11ft high, he should perhaps have refused – a nude statue of Napoleon that graces the stairwell.

These windows face down Rotten Row, the *route du roi* taken by the king from Westminster to the royal hunting forests, and now used by horses exercising riders. Hyde Park, where Henry VIII kept his deer, and played hide-and-seek with Anne Boleyn, is entered through Decimus Burton's fine screen, a welcoming 'Come on in' from the perils of the traffic at Hyde Park Corner.

Serpentine Road, past the bandstand, joins the north bank of the **Serpentine,** created by Queen Caroline in 1830 by damming the Westbourne. George, her husband, would have been cross if he had discovered she had been slipped most of the money to do so by the prime minister! From the bankside beyond the **Dell Café**, look across the water to the Household Cavalry Barracks, which share with the Hilton Hotel responsibility for ruining the park skyline.

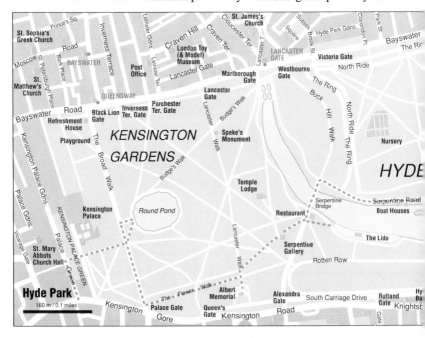

Kensington Gardens and the palace

Between the further bank and the barracks rose the crystal world of the Great International Exhibition of 1851.

Shortly before the bridge is reached, set back against trees on the right and with a formal pool in front is Jacob Epstein's Rima, a memorial to W H Hudson. It was unveiled in 1925 to a tirade of abuse, daubed with green paint and swastikas, but, all passion spent, it survived. The birds, as was intended, like it. Hurry past the fearsome sounding, but rather anonymous Powder Magazine, and enjoy the views from Rennie's beautiful bridge. On its other side are the tents of **Pru Leith's Serpentine Restaurant** (8am–10.30pm; set tea 3–6pm). Beyond is the Lido, where men, women and children can bathe from 6am till dusk in summer.

Cross the road and enter **Kensington Gardens**. You might have been denied the pleasure of access had Queen Caroline had her way and attached the gardens to Kensington Palace. Prime Minister Walpole put her right on the cost – 'Only a Crown, Madam.' The **Serpentine Gallery** stages important exhibitions, but for a real jewel look beyond it to William Kent's delightful **Temple**, then, for a shock contrast in taste, at the **Albert Memorial**, the jewelled shrine to Victoria's consort. It is a potent reminder of the ideals and aspirations of the Victorian age.

Take the Flower Walk to its end in the

Broad Walk; go right for the **Round Pond** opposite Queen Victoria's statue. An entrance to **Kensington Palace** (Monday–Saturday, 9am–5.30pm; Sunday 11–5.30pm), still inhabited by members of the Royal Family, is on the left. The fact that they share it with visitors to the **State Apartments** and the **Court Dress Collection** says a good deal about the changed character of the monarchy. The royal palace had its origins in a private house. After its sale to William III, modest additions were made with the help of Sir Christopher Wren, and later by William Kent for George I.

Just north is the **Orangery** (Monday–Saturday, 10am–5pm; Sunday, noon–5.30pm). Queen Anne liked to have her tea there, and you can too. Another attraction is the sunken 'Dutch' garden near the palace entrance, from its surrounding walk, glimpses of the lily pool are framed between bleached lime trees. A path by the south front of the palace crosses the shady Palace Green and Kensington Palace Gardens. Embassies abound here, often surrounded by interested policemen. Escape can be made to Kensington High Street for buses and the underground.

4. Regent's Park

A visit to London Zoo that takes in some of London's finest Regency architecture; then to Queen Mary's Gardens and finally to Madame Tussaud's and the London Planetarium.

—Start at Great Portland Street Stn, District Line—

Utopian. How else to describe John Nash's conception for the Prince Regent's newly acquired **Marylebone Park**? It was to have a palace, villas for the nobility, terraces of houses for the middle classes, more humble dwellings for the working classes, churches, market and barracks set about a lake, and a river running through a landscaped park. With the exception of the

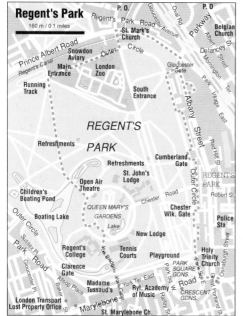

palace, the villas reduced in number from 26 to eight, a single crescent rather than the several planned and the Regent's Canal pressed into service as a river, it's all more or less there.

Get the feel of it by standing on the corner of **Park Crescent**, and imagine the great curve doubled across the Marylebone Road in what would have been Europe's largest circus. Cross the road to Park Square East. In the centre of the terrace is the **Diorama,** where Louis Jacques Daguerre, one of the inventors of photography, opened his entertainment in 1823. Vast paintings, mounted in a rotunda and enhanced by lighting, smoke effects, trompe l'oeil and music, stayed still while the audience moved. Most popular was the landslide that buried a Swiss village. The building faces an uncertain future, but the exhibitions still go on.

In St Andrew's Place is Sir Denys Lasdun's **Royal College of Surgeons**, its lecture theatre resembling nothing so much as a surfacing whale. In the Outer Circle, the Victorian Cambridge Gate is on the site of the Colosseum, which at various times housed a panorama of London viewed from St Paul's dome, marine caverns, and an African glen full of stuffed animals. On the left of **Chester Gate** is a small villa and, mounted on the wall, is the bust of a man with 'round head, snub nose, and little eyes' – Nash's description of himself. He omitted the mischievous grin.

Chester Terrace, long as the Tuileries, is best viewed for its theatrical effect from the park or through the triumphal arches at the ends. Nash and the builder fell out over these. Nash did not want the detached houses that join to the main terrace, but was forced to accept them, finding a happy solution in the triple-arched link. Nash paid special attention to the neighbouring **Cumberland Terrace**, because it would have been the view from the proposed palace, but less to the figures in the pediment, some of which appear to have escaped the overcrowding by taking to the skyline.

Relaxing in Regent's Park

The Royal College of Surgeons *Regent's Park and the Telecom Tower*

Gothic **St Katharine's Hospital** is a refugee from the East End, displaced by the construction of St Katharine's Dock in 1825. Beyond Gloucester Gate turn right and cross Albany Street to **Park Village West**, a garden village of most picturesque villas, especially **Octagon House**, set among trees with delightful gardens on the banks of the now dry canal.

From the village end in Albany Street return to and cross the canal bridge and turn left in Prince Albert Road. Below is the short arm of the canal that led to the **Cumberland Basin** and served the hay market. In the **Gallery Boat** is the promise of Wun Tun Soup, King Prawns War Tat Style and Crispy Aromatic Duck. More promise, too, in the heights of **Primrose Hill** (ahead right),

London Zoo

this time of panoramic views over London, but those with less stamina turn left over the bridge to the Outer Circle and **The Zoo** (daily 9am–5.30pm). The Zoological Society took their bite at the park from the beginning in 1826, and there was some concern that people living there might not like sharing it with lions and leopards. However, its success grew, and in the words of a popular song 'the OK thing to do . . . is toddle to the Zoo'. Unfortunately zoo-going has become less fashionable, and London Zoo has been kept afloat by donations from overseas.

The best time to visit is feeding time, particularly for the chimpanzees and reptiles. Humans are catered for at **Raffles**

Restaurant (he was the founder), and the **Fountain Coffee Shop**.

Tired? A No 274 bus will take you back to Oxford Street or alternatively, you can submit to the lure of green space. Take the first opening left beyond the zoo and the second path from the right to cross the bridge over the lake. It joins the Inner Circle near the Holme. **Queen Mary's Gardens** are the filling in the middle of the circle with the **Open Air Theatre** to the left, and the café entrance to the rose gardens and the water gardens on your right.

Opposite is the York Gate entrance to the park and **St Marylebone Church**, borrowed by Nash as an eye-stopper. Towards Baker Street horrors await you in the waxworks brought from Paris by Marie Tussaud in 1802, but don't be surprised if your favourite pop star has been melted down. Even **Madame Tussaud's** (daily 9am–5.30pm) must move with the times – particularly if it wants to remain London's top attraction. The **London Planetarium** (Monday–Friday, 12.20–5pm; Saturday–Sunday, 10.20am–5pm) is next door, with shows every 40 minutes. Baker Street Station, for the Bakerloo, Metropolitan and Circle lines is just beyond.

5. South Bank

A riverside walk that takes in some of London's most controversial architecture – the Hayward Gallery and the National Theatre complex. Impressionist art at Somerset House and the London that Shakespeare knew.

—Start at Embankment station, Northern and Circle lines—

Shakespeare's Londoners took a boat to the theatre. They had to. The City had banished acting, along with bear- and bull-baiting and brothels, to the south bank of the river. Today's entertainment is a little different, and area offers theatre, music, art, restaurants, cafés, pubs and shops the length of this Thameside boulevard.

Climb the stairs from the **Embankment** to the walkway across the railway bridge from Charing Cross station. The view towards St Paul's is spellbinding and one of the most famous in the city. Come down the other side. The big hall here is the sole survivor of the Festival of Britain of 1951, the **Royal Festival Hall** (foyer exhibitions daily 10am–10pm), victim of a face-lift in the 1960s. Inside are great spaces for grand occasions, changing exhibitions fill the main and upper foyers and the riverside terrace, and there is lunch-time music while you decide which of seven buffets and bars you wish to patronise. There is also an excellent bookshop, and it's all free. Next door is the Queen Elizabeth Hall and the Purcell

The view from the Royal Festival Hall

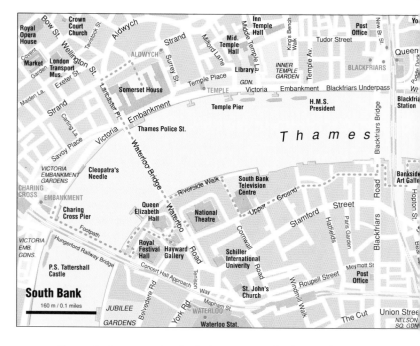

Room, both venues for classical concerts and other performances.

Next door the twinkling neon of the **Hayward Gallery** (daily 10am–6pm) signals yet another major art exhibition in its concrete bunker. This is London's most mainstream venue for contemporary art. Outside there is more than a hint of Paris in the bookstalls under **Waterloo Bridge**, and here also, two temples to cinema – the **National Film Theatre** (day membership available) and the fascinating **Museum of the Moving Image** (daily 10am–6pm), complete with actors in costume who wander through the exhibits. Under the arches here down-and-outs live in their cardboard city.

Culture extends a long hand over Waterloo Bridge. On the north bank is **Somerset House**, lately wrested from the civil servants and blessed with a transplant from Bloomsbury, the **Courtauld Collection** (Monday–Saturday, 10am–6pm; Sunday 2–6pm). Much loved familiars, such as Van Gogh, Gauguin, Cézanne, da Vinci and Rembrandt are all included in this exceptional, personal collection.

Back on the South Bank, the **Royal National Theatre** consists of three theatres, and nine bars and buffets. Continue on the riverside way. Coin Street market is interesting. The OXO tower forces a diversion until **Blackfriars Bridge**. Cross the approach road to Bankside and skirt the power station. Wren watched the building of St Paul's from a house here, perhaps the **Cardinal's Cap**. The dwelling on the alley is a successor to a notorious inn, the Cardinal's Hat – maybe named after Cardinal Wolsey.

Bear Gardens led to the 'baiting ring', new in 1550. Sixty years later it was replaced by the Hope, where Ben Jonson's *Bartholomew Fair* was first produced. See all about it in the **Bear Gardens Museum** (Monday–Saturday, 10am–5pm; Sunday, 2–5.30pm). Just by the arch of Southwark Bridge is the original site of the Globe the-

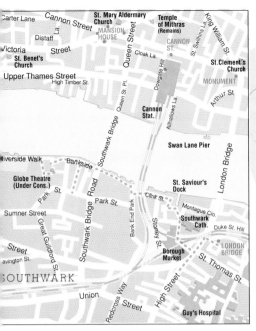

atre, built in 1599 with Shakespeare as shareholder and actor. Nearby a replica of the Globe is almost completed.

At Bank End, by the railway viaduct, is the friendly **Anchor** (barbecue Monday–Friday, noon–3pm, 5.30–9.30pm; Saturday–Sunday noon–9.30pm), corner post of the Barclay Perkins Brewery. Little has changed here in over 200 years. Beyond the dark arches lay the Bishop of Winchester's 13th-century town residence, its surviving fragments trapped in the fabric of Victorian warehouses, now revealed in the beauty of the banqueting hall's rose window. The bishop's notorious prison, 'The Clink', gave its name to the street and the slang term for prison. 'Material of an explicit nature' is shown in the **Clink Exhibition** (daily 10am–6pm; shorter hours in Winter). Time was when parishioners could land goods free of toll at St Mary Overy Dock, or have their wives put in the ducking stool. A three-masted schooner, the **Kathleen and May** (daily 11am–4pm), now fills the dock. Good river views from the terrace or the pub, the **Old Thameside Inn**.

Southwark Cathedral is something of a treasure house of church relics. A churchwarden's son, christened here in 1607, founded Harvard University, partly with money from the sale of the Queen's Head in Borough High Street, one of the many galleried inns that lined the approach to London Bridge. Of these only the **George** still exists. Scrubbed wood, blackened paint, open hearth and galleried yard evoke the 1670s. London Bridge station is a short walk north.

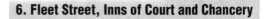

6. Fleet Street, Inns of Court and Chancery

To Fleet Street where the pubs remain even if the journalists have gone; try one, then stroll through the Inns of Court and visit the extraordinary Sir John Soane's Museum, then the British Museum.

—*Ludgate Circus. Bus from Charing Cross*—

Walk up Fleet Street from Ludgate Circus and you are following the west bank of the old Fleet River, now unceremoniously buried in a sewer. You are also following in the footsteps of generations of journalists and lawyers; the newspapermen have now departed, but the lawyers remain.

On the left, the narrow Bride's Avenue reveals the steeple of **St Bride's church**, Wren's tallest and the inspiration for the first tiered wedding-cake. He rebuilt the church after the Great Fire of London in 1666. It was gutted in the Blitz of 1940, and restored to a new, rather than former, glory. The fascinating **Crypt Museum** (daily 8.15am–5.30pm) is a magpie collection of Roman mosaics, Saxon church walls and William Caxton's *Ovid*.

Across the street, the striking building of black glass and chromium was the brain-centre of Express Newspapers until the 1980s exodus of national newspapers from Fleet Street to cheaper high-tech sites. The pillared palace a few metres further on used to house the *Daily Telegraph*; bankers now inhabit it. Look out for **Wine Office Court**, one of the warren of alleys on this side. Here is the **Cheshire Cheese** pub (rebuilt 1667), no doubt known to Dr Samuel Johnson and his cronies, among them Oliver Goldsmith, who lived at No 6. Well-signposted is **Dr Johnson's House** in

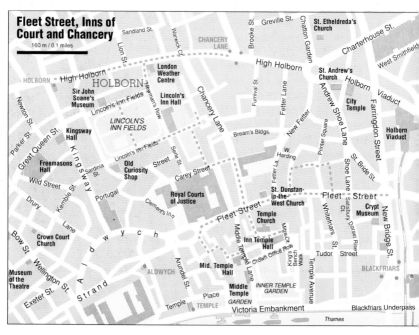

Fleet Street, Inns of Court and Chancery

160 m / 0.1 miles

Gough Square (weekdays May–September, 11am–5.30pm; October–April, 11am–5pm). Johnson lived here from 1748 to 1759, working on his dictionary in the garret with six poor copyists. Back in Fleet Street, across the road at No 47 is **El Vino's**, a self-important wine bar, once a journalists' haunt and scene of feminist skirmishes because it won't serve women at the bar.

Just beyond Fetter Lane, on the right, is **St Dunstan-in-the-West**, and its 17th-century clock with striking jacks. Over the porch at the side is a lifelike statue of Queen Elizabeth I. When Lud Gate was removed it was brought here together with King Lud and his sons, who loiter in the shadows below. A little further on is the gatehouse entrance to **Clifford's Inn** with the chequered arms of the de Cliffords over the arch, and, beyond, a quiet oasis of trees and grass. **Coutts & Co**. is the bank where Queen Elizabeth II keeps her money. On the south side, at 1 Fleet Street, is **Child & Co**, England's oldest private bank (now part of Royal Bank of Scotland).

Just before Child is the half-timbered gateway to Middle Temple Lane and the quadrangles and courts, chambers and flower gardens of what resembles an Oxford college. This is the **Temple**, the heart of legal London. On the first floor of the Inner Temple Gateway of 1611 is **Prince Henry's Room** (10am–1pm, 2–4pm), with the initials of James I's son on the elaborate ceiling. Enter the lane beneath and turn left for the **Temple Church**.

Keep left to King's Bench Walk and turn right in front of Paper Buildings past the gardens running down to the Embankment. In Middle Temple Lane turn right and take the steps left, past the Hall, to Fountain Court. Go through the gate to Devereux Court. In **The Devereux**, the old 'Grecian Coffee House', Addison, Steele and Goldsmith met. Past the **Edgar Wallace**, named after the master detective story writer, is Essex Street. Turn right and you emerge on the Strand, facing the imposing **Law Courts**. Turn right and cross the street, turning into Chancery Lane, whose eating-places include **Wheeler's** fish restaurant, **Hodgson's Restaurant and Wine Bar**, and **Chez Gérard's**.

In **Carey Street,** on the left, is the **Silver Mousetrap** jewellers

(established 1690) and the **Seven Stars** pub (1602), the 'Magpie and Stump' of Dickens's *Pickwick Papers*. Enter **Lincoln's Inn** through the arch of Back Gate. Walk through New Square with Old Buildings on your right to **Old Hall**, built in the fifth year of Henry VII, and the **Chapel** (Monday–Friday, noon–2.30pm). Return to New Square and the exit gate to the Fields.

Sir John Soane's Museum (Tuesday–Saturday, 10am–5pm, admission free), is at number 13 on the north side of the square. It is one of London's little-known gems, its maze of rooms packed with antiquities and paintings, including Hogarth's *Rake's Progress* and *The Election*. Highly recommended.

This miniature museum serves as an appetiser for the magnificent **British Museum** (Monday–Saturday, 10am–5pm; Sunday, 2.30–6pm), 10 minutes' walk away (exit Lincoln's Inn Fields via Great Turnstile to High Holborn; turn left, pass Holborn tube station and cross the road; take the third turn right into Museum Street). You could explore the British Museum for days; but, if pressed, don't miss the 'Elgin' Marbles and the Anglo-Saxon jewellery from the Sutton Hoo ship burial.

7. St Paul's and Smithfield

St Paul's, Christopher Wren's magnificent cathedral, Smithfield meat market, London's oldest hospital, medieval alleys and memorials to the Knights of St John and Karl Marx.

—*Start at St Paul's station, Central Line*—

On 29 December 1940 St Paul's Cathedral held its breath. A year into World War II it was ringed with fire as bombs rained down on the heart of London. Miraculously it survived, a symbol of a nation's resistance. The spire of its Gothic predecessor had succumbed to fire in 1561, and upkeep deteriorated. Inigo Jones gave the west front a facelift, but it was the Great Fire of London that hastened the decision to rebuild, with Wren embarking a solution to the problem in 1672. His magnificent wooden model, now in the

St Paul's Cathedral

cathedral Library, was rejected and what we see today was his reluctant compromise.

Back in Newgate Street, cross and walk left to Giltspur Street, which leads to West Smithfield, which has had more than its share of the rough of London history, including public executions and burnings, the slaughter of cattle and sheep driven into market, and St Bartholomew's Fair, which foundered on vice and violence in 1840. At the ringside are London's oldest hospital, St Bartholomew's, and its next oldest church, St Bartholomew-the-Great, both founded on the highest humanitarian and religious ideals by Henry I's jester, Rahere.

Bart's Gatehouse, with Henry VIII in a niche, looks more like the entrance to a college quad than a hospital. Walk through to where, on the left, is the hospital church, **St Bartholomew-the-Less**, a Gothic octagon of 1823 sitting happily with a medieval tower. Outside, turn right to the 13th-century arch of the gatehouse to **St Bartholomew-the-Great**, its half-timbering hidden until a World War I bomb revealed all. Enter the church and you are in the Norman chancel of the demolished nave of the Augustinian Priory. Prior Bolton's oriel window high in the south side enabled him to drop in on proceedings unobserved. A much abused building, it suffered a printing works in the Lady Chapel, and in the north transept the stonework is darkened from a blacksmith's forge.

No 41 Cloth Fair, overlooking the graveyard, gives a very good idea of what London looked like before the Great Fire. John Betjeman described his house on the corner opposite as 'the nicest place to live in' before the night-time roar of the refrigerator trucks drove him out. A little further on a passage takes you to Long Lane and **Ye Olde Red Cow**, home of 'Hot Toddy'. Early starts for meat porters on cold mornings call for desperate measures, and keep Smithfield pubs and cafés open 24 hours a day.

Cross to Lindsey Street and to Charterhouse Square. The **Charterhouse** (tours, Wednesday, April–July, 2.45 pm), first a Carthusian Priory founded in 1371, became a manor house for the Duke

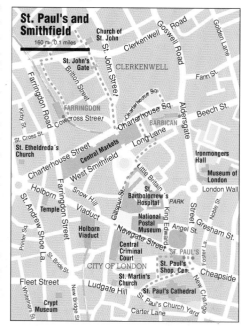

Charterhouse, the gatehouse

of Norfolk, and, later, coal-owner Thomas Sutton's 'hospital' for poor brethren, a school for poor boys, then later, the public school famous for the quality of its education. The brethren are still there, bachelors and widows of pensionable age. Left of the gatehouse is the **Fox and Anchor pub**, with its long and famous tradition of serving delicious wood-smoked Scottish haddock, but only on Wednesday!

Turn right into St John Street, fork left into St John's Lane and walk back 400 years to the Gatehouse of the Priory of St John of Jerusalem. Elizabeth I's Master of Revels had his office here, the *Gentleman's Magazine* was published here, and before it was taken over by the Order of St John of Jerusalem it was a pub.

Cross Clerkenwell Road to St John's Square, once the courtyard of the priory. Jerusalem Passage leads to Aylesbury Street and Clerkenwell Green. At the tarmacked end of the Green is the elegant **Sessions House** of 1782. Full marks to the Masons for its rescue. There is a good pub in the **Crown,** which has a Conspirators' Clock in the bar, commemorating the unsuccessful attempt on the life of Charles II. Facing the Green is the **Marx Memorial Library** (Monday, Friday, 2–6pm; Tuesday–Thursday, 2–9pm; Saturday 11am–1pm). The first of the Tolpuddle Martyrs to return home addressed a mass demonstration here in 1838, and in 1892 the first socialist press was set up in this building. In a tiny corner office, Lenin edited *Iskra* – 'The Spark' that was to kindle the Russian Revolution. Farringdon station is left down Farringdon Road.

St Paul's at dusk　　　　　　　　　　　　　　　*Sunset in Hyde Park*

Shopping

London is a consumer's paradise where simply window-shopping can be fun. Shopping is divided into different areas, each with its own individual character.

Oxford Street and Regent Street

Oxford Street is England's principal high street and is always crowded. All the major high street fashion chains such as **Next**, **C&A** and **Top Shop** are here. There are also large branches of **Virgin** and HMV Records. There are several department stores of which **Selfridges** is the most notable. The Marble Arch Branch of **Marks and Spencer** is the flagship of this leading British chain store with its own renowned brand of quality clothes for the whole family. The recent recession has taken Oxford Street rather downmarket.

Opposite Bond Street tube is a discreet little alleyway leading to St Christopher's Place where a cluster of trendy shops have grouped together. Meanwhile, on the other side of Oxford Street, is fashion-

Oxford Circus

able South Molton Street which moves in the direction of Bond Street both geographically and in its range of up-market fashion boutiques. Stores such as **Browns** stock collections from major international designers. Close by in Brook Street are **Roland Klein, Antony Price, Commes des Garçons** and **Gianfranco Ferre**.

Serious shopping along Regent Street begins at Oxford Circus with **Dickins and Jones**, a classy fashion store for those with a more mature and refined taste. Next door is the distinctive mock Tudor frontage of **Liberty**, famous for its exquisite printed fabrics. Nearby, **Hamleys** proudly proclaims itself to be the world's largest toy shop. Moving on towards Piccadilly you will come across exclusive jewellers **Mappin & Webb** and **Garrard & Co** (jewellers to the Queen) and the fine china stores of **Waterford, Wedgwood** and **Villeroy & Boch**. **Jaeger**, **Austin Reed** and **Aquascutum** are good for classic English clothes and country casuals.

Bond Street and Mayfair

Bond Street has a long-standing tradition of offering the best money can buy, and if any of London's streets are paved with gold it must surely be this one. In this vicinity can be found over 400 of the world's most élite fine art and antique galleries, plus leading auction houses, exquisite jewellers such as **Tiffany** and **Cartier** and leading international couturiers, **Valentino**, **Chanel** and **Lagerfeld** amongst many others. A peek in the window of **Asprey's** will reveal the most decadent gifts in town. Running parallel to Old Bond Street is the elegant Burlington Arcade (see Walk 3: *West End*), lined with small exclusive shops, many selling quality British-made goods.

St James's and Piccadilly

This area, which is littered with gentlemen's clubs, is steeped in tradition and the 'old order'. Here is a concentration of old-fashioned gentlemen's outfitters with the hand-tailored suits of Savile Row and the made-to-measure shirts of Jermyn Street. In timeless St James's Street are shoemaker **John Lobb** and fine hat maker **James Lock** whilst in Jermyn Street, **George F Trumper**

The Edwardian food halls at Harrods

supplies traditional toiletries to the aristocracy and **Floris** provides them with delicious fragrances. The Dickensian wine merchants, **Berry Bros & Rudd** at 3 St James's Street, have a cellar stocked with rare wines. **Fortnum and Mason** on Piccadilly have been supplying the English gentry with exotic and unusual groceries for centuries. For the traditional English look, **Simpson** at 203 Piccadilly has several floors of garments for men and women.

Knightsbridge

Harrods, on the Brompton Road, dominates the scene of exclusive and high fashion shopping in Knightsbridge. One of the world's largest and most famous department stores, no-one should miss the fabulous displays in the Edwardian tiled food halls. Close by is pretty Beauchamp Place with its small chic boutiques including **Caroline Charles** and **The Emmanuels** (famous for Princess Diana's wedding dress). **Emporio Armani** also adds to the prestige of this absorbing stretch of the Brompton Road. Sloane Street has become the centre for high fashion in London with many world class designers.

King's Road and Fulham

Despite rising overheads, which have caused many of the distinctive independent boutiques to disappear, the King's Road is still good for trendy street fashion. Shops such as **Jones**, **Fiorucci**, **Boy**, and **The Garage** indoor market are dotted between Sloane Square and **Vivienne Westwood's** wacky World's End store at No 430. This end of the King's Road has shoe designer **Johnny Moke** and several period clothes shops, from the 1950s college style of **American Classics** to the English retro look of **Twentieth Century Box**.

The King's Road and Fulham are also well known for their fashionable interior furnishing shops such as the **Designers Guild** and **Timney Fowler**. A large number of dealers in fine period furniture, as well as antique markets, such as **Chenil Galleries** and **Antiquarius** are scattered along the length of the King's Road.

The Conran Shop, housed within the beautiful Art Nouveau tiled Michelin Building at 81 Fulham Road, is a unique and stylish showroom selling designer furniture and household accessories. The stylish fashion of **Joseph**, **Jasper Conran** and others have also taken residence here at the beginning of the chic Fulham Road. Back in Sloane Square, Chelsea's only department store, **Peter Jones**, is particularly good for household furnishings and appliances at unbeatable prices.

Soho and Carnaby Street

Much of the sleaze of old Soho has been swept away to be replaced by wild and trendy fashion

Gerrard Street in busy Chinatown

shops. Despite Carnaby Street's downhill spiral following the 'swinging Sixties', a spirit of innovation still flourishes in its neighbouring streets. Here are the likes of **Pam Hogg**, **Academy Soho**, and **Boyd & Storey** in Newburgh Street and **Young Gaultier** in Fouberts Place. Soho can also offer the original and quirky menswear of **Christopher New** (Dean Street), the folklore-based garments of **Workers For Freedom** (Lower John Street) and the ultimate in casual street fashion for men from **The Duffer of St George** (D'Arblay Street).

Several old Italian delicatessens such as **Fratelli Camisa** in Berwick Street and **Lina Stores** in Brewer Street are still standing their ground, survivors of an era when Soho was far more continental. Meanwhile, Chinatown, which is centred around Gerrard Street, is the obvious place for the best Chinese groceries.

Kensington High Street

Although largely inhabited by chain stores this area is still good for street fashion. **Kensington market** is full of stalls selling leather jackets and all the latest hip gear whilst across the road the more prestigious **Hyper-Hyper** has stalls of imaginative clothes and accessories by adventurous young designers.

Away from the hustle and bustle of the High Street is Kensington Church Street with some of London's finest, and most expensive, antique shops, dealing in everything from fine art originals through to porcelain.

Covent Garden

Within the narrow streets and piazzas of this characterfully redeveloped area, once London's main fruit and vegetable market, many interesting craft and gift shops and stalls have taken root. Covent Garden also offers the designer wear of **Paul Smith**, **Jones** and **Michiko Koshino** as well as leading fashion chains such as **Jigsaw**, **Whistles**, **Hobbs**, **Woodhouse** and **Blazer**.

Several good, though rather expensive, period clothes shops can be found around Neal Street and Monmouth Street. For designer household accessories there are **Artemide** and **Astrohome**. The quaint Neal's Yard is a centre for organic wholefood with its own bakery, dairy, grocer, apothecary, cheese specialist and wholefood warehouse. Opposite Neal's Yard is a smart and sophisticated new shopping centre, **Thomas Neal's**, full of interesting ideas.

On Long Acre is **Stanford's** map and travel bookshop and **Dillons Art Bookshop**, whilst nearby, Charing Cross Road is a haven for bookworms. It is crowded with bookshops ranging from **Foyles**, the largest and most confusing, to the small antiquarian establishments of Cecil Court, a little pedestrian street towards Trafalgar Square.

Street Markets

For antiques, bric-a-brac, period clothes and general junk try **Portobello Road** W11 (Saturday) where many antique dealers do their shopping. As a result the stall-holders know exactly what they are selling, and the prices reflect this, though there is still the chance of a bargain if you really know your stuff. **Camden Lock** NW1 (Saturday–Sunday) is very popular as a weekend attraction. However its wares are not cheap, and its success means that parts of it have attracted the attention of redevelopers. For (quite pricey) antiques visit pretty **Camden Passage** N1 (Wednesday and Saturday) and the very early morning **Bermondsey Square** dealers-market in SE1 (Friday).

For food, **Berwick Street** and **Rupert Street** (see Day 1: *Covent Garden and Soho*) in the heart of Soho are bustling weekday markets selling perhaps the best fruit and vegetables London has to offer, whilst **Leadenhall Market** EC3, located within the beautiful old Victorian covered market from which it derived its name (it had lead roofing at a time when other markets in the city were thatched) is good for quality meat, poultry and fish, despite having been gentrified and revived to attract modern City workers.

Of the other major City markets, Billingsgate, described as being the home of fresh fish and foul language, has moved to Docklands; Smithfield meat market still functions, although there are plans to move it, and Spitalfields fruit and vegetable market is now heavily organic and craft-based. The original has gone to Hackney Marshes.

Restaurants

London is one of the great culinary cities of the world. This is partly due to the breadth of cosmopolitan cuisines available, but also to the re-evaluation over recent years of the indigenous cuisine of the British. Innovative chefs have injected new life into traditional English recipes, enriching them with French and ethnic influences. However, the traditional practices of Sunday lunch, roast carveries and fish and chips are still very much part of the scene, as is 'afternoon tea', which is served in many hotels.

The main concentration of London's restaurants is in the West End with Soho providing the most interesting and widest choice, whilst Covent Garden can offer good pre-theatre suppers. Chinatown, centring around Gerrard Street, is full of Cantonese restaurants. Bayswater also has many good value ethnic restaurants. A good meal out in London can be expensive, reflecting the high cost

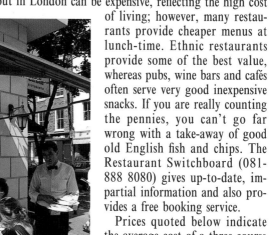

of living; however, many restaurants provide cheaper menus at lunch-time. Ethnic restaurants provide some of the best value, whereas pubs, wine bars and cafés often serve very good inexpensive snacks. If you are really counting the pennies, you can't go far wrong with a take-away of good old English fish and chips. The Restaurant Switchboard (081-888 8080) gives up-to-date, impartial information and also provides a free booking service.

Prices quoted below indicate the average cost of a three-course meal for two with a bottle of house wine.

Traditional British

SIMPSONS-IN-THE-STRAND
100 Strand WC2 (071-836 9112). The Grand Divan Tavern is an Edwardian dining room renowned for serving the best roast beef in London. Staunchly traditional. Formal dress. *£51.*

THE QUALITY CHOP HOUSE
94 Farringdon Road EC1 (071-837 5093). A 19th-century City clerks' dining room with its original fixed wooden seating intact. The food has gone up-market with the likes of blue fish with fennel sauce on the menu beside plain lamb chops. *£38.*

Modern British

ALASTAIR LITTLE
49 Frith Street W1 (071-734 5183). Doyen of the new school of British cooking: imaginative and eclectic food within tasteful surroundings. *£70.*

BABOON, JASON COURT
76 Wigmore Street W1 (071-224 2992). Serves superb, well thought-out modern British food based around traditional recipes. *£65.*

Sunday Lunch

WILSON'S
236 Blythe Road W14 (071-603 7267). One of the best Sunday lunches in town, with consistently high quality throughout the week in this dignified restaurant, where the patron may be seen in a kilt. *£40 lunch/£57 dinner.*

THE ENGLISH HOUSE
3 Milner Street SW3 (071-584 3002). Quaint chintzy English dining room within a pretty Chelsea town house. The food has flair and an historic influence. *£35 lunch/£55 dinner. (*Sister restaurant to **THE LINDSAY HOUSE**, *21 Romilly Street W1.)*

American Theme

HARD ROCK CAFÉ
150 Old Park Lane W1 (071-629 0382). Part of the world-wide chain, this was one of the first. A shrine to rock music, housing a collection of rock memorabilia. Serves some of the best burgers in town. Noisy with long queues but great fun. *£30.*

ROCK ISLAND DINER
London Pavilion, Piccadilly Circus W1 (071-287 5500). Fun and loud 1950s-style diner kitted out with kitsch décor, a resident DJ and dancing waitresses and barmen. *£25.*

Chinese

FUNG SHING

15 Lisle Street W1 (071-437 1539).
Has long been one of the best restaurants in Chinatown and is consequently always packed. If it is full, there are plenty of other choices. *£40.*

WONG KEI

41–43 Wardour Street W1 (071-437 8408). Regular crowds aren't deterred by the rude service for which this restaurant's waiters are famed. Huge, with three floors, serving good cheap Cantonese food. Cash only. *Under £20.*

Fish

RUDLAND AND STUBBS

35–37 Greenhill Rents, Cowcross Street EC1 (071-253 0148). Theis restaurant serves English and French-style fish dishes, including several types of oyster in season, in an old-fashioned setting of tiled walls and bare floorboards, near Smithfield meat market. *£37.*

SEA SHELL FISH BAR

49 Lisson Grove NW1 (071-723 8703). A renowned fish and chip restaurant and take-away (carry-out). Although, as this traditional

English delicacy goes (the cheapest meal on the high street), the restaurant is expensive. Its wide choice of fish is consistently very fresh and well cooked. *£25.*

French

L'ARTISTE ASSOIFFÉ

122 Kensington Park Road W11 (071-727 5111). Carousel horses and caged parrots adorn this delightful and entertaining restaurant close to Portobello's antique shops. Good after a day's shopping. *£40.*

GAVVERS

61 Lower Sloane Street SW1 (071-730 5983). Related to LE GAVROCHE (see 'Top Chefs'), Gavvers operates set menus providing quality combined with attentive service in comfortable surroundings. Aperitif, three-course dinner, half bottle of wine, after-dinner coffee, and service all included in the bill. *£27 per person.*

Greek

ELYSEE

13 Percy Street W1 (071-636 4804). One of several Greek restaurants in this area that can offer an action-packed evening of plate smashing, live music and belly dancing. This one has outdoor seating for those rare summer evenings. *£45.*

Indian

BOMBAY BRASSERIE

Bailey's Hotel, Courtfield Close, SW7 (071 370 4040). Stylish decor harks back to the days of the Raj. Try to get a table in the conservatory. *£60*

KHAN'S

13 Westbourne Grove W2 (071-727 5420). This large colonial style dining-room is famous for its value. Crowded in the evenings, the atmosphere is that of constant bustle. *£25 per person.*

THE RED FORT
77 Dean Street W1 (071-437 2410).
Respected Soho venue which offers
superb Mogul cooking in comfortably
luxurious surroundings. Long-stayer
in the London scene. *£45.*

Italian
LA FAMIGLIA
*7 Langton Street SW10 (071-351
0761).* Successful restaurant with
pleasant food and décor done the
southern Italian way. Large outdoor
eating area. *£40.*

ORSO
*27 Wellington Street WC2 (071-240
5269).* Fashionable with the theatre
crowd, Orso is set in a basement with
simple décor and authentic northern
Italian food. *£50.*

PIZZA EXPRESS
10 Dean Street W1 (071-437 9595).
One of a trendy and civilised chain
throughout London, this branch has
the added attraction of jazz in the
basement. The classiest is PIZZA ON
THE PARK, *13 Knightsbridge,* and the
most fashionable is KETTNER'S, *29
Romilly Street.* £25.

Japanese
AJIMURA
51–53 Shelton Street WC2 (071-240
0178). Certainly one of the most rea-
sonably priced Japanese restaurants in
London. Lunch and pre-theatre set
menus are best value. *£35.*

IKEDA
30 Brook Street W1 (071-629 2730).
Sit at the Yakitori and Sushi bars to
get the best from the Japanese experience at this small and friendly Mayfair
restaurant. *£70 (set lunch £12).*

Malaysian
THE PENANG
41 Hereford Road W2 (071-229 2982).
Good food with a home-cooked fresh-
ness at this friendly, small and unas-
suming restaurant. *£30.*

Mexican
CAFÉ PACIFICO
5 Langley Street WC2 (071-379 7728).
Young and noisy Tex Mex joint
housed within a converted Covent
Garden warehouse. *£30.*

Middle Eastern
MAROUSH II
*38 Beauchamp Place SW3 (071-581
5434).* Popular with Middle Eastern
high rollers who congregate here after
a night on the town. Excellent Leban-
ese food. Last orders 5.30am. *£40.*

Russian

BORSCHT 'N' TEARS
46 Beauchamp Place SW3 (071-589 5003). Zany Russian restaurant with a sense of humour that attracts a predominantly young clienteley. *£35.*

Spanish

COSTA DORADA
47–55 Hanway Street W1 (071-631 5117). Lively restaurant-cum-tapas bar where the action goes on well into the night with flamenco dancing accompanied by live music. *£50.*

Thai

CHIANG MAI
48 Frith Street W1 (071-437 7444). Modelled on a traditional stilt house with an extensive menu of good northern Thai cuisine. *£30.*

Vegetarian

MILDRED'S
58 Greek Street W1 (071-494 1634). Imaginative cooking, well presented in café-style surroundings. Vegan options. *£13 (bring your own wine).*

THAI GARDEN
249 Globe Road E2 (081-981 5748). Best vegetarian restaurant in the 1991 *Time Out* Eating & Drinking Awards.

Places to be Seen

THE IVY
1 West Street WC2 (071-836 4751). High quality décor, gallery-worthy art, and well thought out food have made for the successful regeneration of The Ivy, which re-opened its doors in 1990. *£60.* Its stylish relative, LE CAPRICE, *Arlington Street SW1,* is also very fashionable.

KENSINGTON PLACE
201 Kensington Church Street W8 (071-727 3184). Trendy and informal, this New York-style restaurant is always busy. The décor is modernist and the food is adventurous. *£55.*

LANGAN'S BRASSERIE
Stratton Street W1 (071-491 8822). Langan's large reputation for attracting celebrities often overshadows the food. Michael Caine is part owner of this fashionable brasserie. *£50.*

Top Chefs

CHEZ NICO
90 Park Lane, W1 (071-409 1290). A passionate perfectionist, Nico Ladenis serves classic French cuisine earning him two Michelin stars. *£100+.*

LE GAVROCHE
43 Upper Brook Street W1 (071-408 0881). The only London restaurant ever to have been awarded three Mich-

elin stars, thanks to the excellence of Albert Roux. *£100+*.

HARVEY'S
2 Bellevue Road SW17 (081-672 0114). Marco Pierre White has been replaced by Kelvin Davies, a young chef from New Zealand. Cuisine with a Californian/Mediterranean accent. *£70+*.

THE INN ON THE PARK, the CAPITAL and the CONNAUGHT hotels all feature restaurants which have excellent chefs; each one has a Michelin star.

Drinks (with food)

BAR DES AMIS DU VIN
11–13 Hanover Place WC2 (071-379 3444). Dark, atmospheric basement bar with a good selection of wine and decent French snacks.

CAFÉ PELICAN
45 St Martin's Lane WC2 (071-379 0309). Chic brasserie popular with the theatre crowd serving a good repertoire of French food. Winner in the Best Service category of the 1991 *Time Out* Eating & Drinking Awards.

MARKET BAR
240a Portobello Road W11 (071-229 6472). A triumph of the art of the distressed interior in the shell of an old pub. Fashionable retreat away from the bustling market.

Cocktail Bars

AMERICAN BAR
Savoy Hotel, Strand WC2 (071-836 4343). London's most classic cocktail bar within the sophisticated Savoy Hotel. Jacket and tie.

RUMOURS
33 Wellington Street WC2 (071-836 0038). Huge, popular and lively, this is a modern bar with an endless list of cocktails, where the punters get crushed along with the ice.

Notable Pubs

THE ANCHOR
1 Bankside SE1 (riverside).

THE BLACK FRIAR
174 Queen Victoria Street EC4.

THE DICKENS INN
St Katharine's Way E1 (riverside).

YE OLDE CHESHIRE CHEESE
145 Fleet Street EC4.

THE SPANIARD'S INN
Hampstead Lane NW3.

THE DOVE
19 Upper Mall W6 (riverside).

West End Theatres

London's theatreland centres around Shaftesbury Avenue and Covent Garden where some shows have been running for decades.

West End theatres are popular and tickets may be hard to obtain. If you can't book through the theatre box office (credit card bookings by telephone accepted) try Ticketmaster (071-344 4444) and First Call (071-240 7200) before going to other agencies who may charge a hefty fee. Avoid touts, as they will inevitably try to rip you off and sometimes have forged tickets.

The SWET (Society of West End Theatres) ticket office in Leicester Square has tickets available at half-price on the day, from noon for

matinees and from 2pm for evening performances. Be prepared for long queues. Some theatres keep back a number of tickets for each performance to sell at the box office from 10am on the day. Consult the listings in the weekly *Time Out* magazine or quality newspapers for what's on in the West End and the many fringe theatres around London.

Classical Music

Main Venues
BARBICAN HALL
Silk Street EC2 (071-638 8891). Home to the London Symphony Orchestra.

ROYAL ALBERT HALL
Kensington Gore SW7 (071-589 8212) Hosts 'The Proms' every summer.

ROYAL FESTIVAL HALL
South Bank SE1 (071-928 8800). The most important classical music venue.

WIGMORE HALL
36 Wigmore Street W1 (071-935 2141). Excellent for chamber concerts.

Ballet & Opera

Main Venues

THE COLISEUM
St Martin's Lane WC2 (071-836 3161). Home to the English National Opera with performances from the Royal Festival Ballet and other major companies in the summer months.

THE ROYAL OPERA HOUSE
Bow Street WC2 (071-240 1066). Traditional home of the Royal Opera and Ballet. Operas sung in their original language. Dressy affair.

THE SADLER'S WELLS/LILIAN BAYLIS THEATRE
Rosebery Avenue EC1 (071-278 8916). Opera and all styles of dance are represented by major dance companies.

Nightclubs

Many nightclubs feature 'one-nighters' which centre around a particular style or scene. Consult *Time Out* for full details. Dress codes can be strict, so make sure you look the part.

EQUINOX DISCOTHEQUE
Leicester Square WC2 (071-437 1446). Huge disco, famous for its light show; this is one of the biggest discos in Europe, attracting a young crowd in smart casual dress. *£6–10.*

THE FRIDGE
Town Hall Parade, Brixton Hill SW2 (071-326 5100). The coolest and hippest venue south of the river; renowned for spectacular one-nighters. Worth seeking out. *£5–8.*

HEAVEN
Villiers Street WC2 (071-839 3852). Beneath Charing Cross development is one of the best dance clubs in town. Gay men only on Wednesday, Saturday. Relaxed dress code. *£4–8.*

HIPPODROME
Charing Cross Road WC2 (071-437 4311). Incorporates all the technological tricks you would expect from a discothèque of the 1990s. Popular with celebrities. Smart. *£4–10.*

LACEY'S
80–81 St Martin's Lane WC2 (071-240 8187). Mainstream disco with strict dress code. Downstairs bar has a pianist and live jazz music every night. Smart. *£10.*

LEGENDS
29 Old Burlington Street W1 (071-437 9933). Glossy Mayfair club which attracts a crowd who like to dress up and try out crazy dance moves. Hosts a variety of one-nighters. Hip. *£5–9.*

LIMELIGHT

136 Shaftesbury Avenue W1 (071-434 0572). A converted church; if you worship music, then the sound system will put you in touch with heaven. *£10.*

SAMANTHA'S

3 New Burlington Street W1 (071-734 6249). Mainstream disco that has been around for a long time. Attracts well-dressed and more mature clubbers. Smart. *£3–6.*

SHAFTESBURY'S

24 Shaftesbury Avenue W1 (071-734 2017). Mainstream disco with champagne bar and brasserie. Not as hip as others, but has the occasional trendy one-nighter. *£8–£15.*

STRINGFELLOWS

16 Upper St Martin's Lane WC2 (071-240 5534). Popular location for the *paparazzi* and victims who still seem to frequent the place. Strong on glamour. *£8–£15.*

SUBTERANIA

12 Acklam Road, Ladbroke Grove W10 (081-960 4590). Well-designed modern interior, hewn out of the concrete of the Westway. A refreshing addition to London's club scene. Casual. *£5–7.*

WAG CLUB

35 Wardour Street W1 (071-437 5534). Soho club open until 6am at weekends. Heavy duty dance music and fresh fruit bar to keep you going. Hip. *£5–£10.*

Cabaret

MADAME JO JO'S

8–10 Brewer Street W1 (071-734 2473). Lacking the sleaze and daring associated with Soho's past, Madame Jo Jo's still offers one of the best late-night outings in London with captivating cabaret shows provided by leggy male lovelies in amazing glitzy costumes.

THE COMEDY STORE

1 Oxendon Street, W1 (0426-914433). A night at this well-established stand-up venue will remind you that comedy need not always be accompanied by canned laughter. On a good night the comedians in the audience are as famous as those on stage.

Jazz

100 CLUB

100 Oxford Street W1 (071-636 0933). Basic décor and two bars serving drinks at pub prices, this is a renowned venue for live jazz and rhythm-and-blues from established bands and young unknowns alike.

BASS CLEF

35 Coronet Street N1 (071-729 2476). Cramped basement club hosting popular jazz through the week, soul on Monday, Latin and Salsa on Friday and African dance music on Saturday. Also the Tenor Clef, upstairs.

DOVER STREET WINE BAR

8–9 Dover Street W1 (071-629 9813). Intimate basement where you can dine by candlelight whilst being entertained with live jazz, soul or R&B. Until 3am. Popular with singles.

RONNIE SCOTT'S

47 Frith Street W1 (071-439 0747). London's most famous jazz venue where food and service are less of an attraction than the music, atmosphere and indeed Ronnie Scott himself who opens up the evening's entertainment with his infamous 'jokes'. Arrive early as it gets very crowded, especially at weekends.

DAY TRIPS

Greenwich Time

A trip down the river to the 'village' of Greenwich for the Maritime Museum and Royal Observatory.

—Take a boat from Westminster or Charing Cross Pier—

Queen Elizabeth I took her state barge from Whitehall Stairs to be rowed downstream to her palace at Greenwich. With less pomp and more comfort, a boat from **Charing Cross Pier**, only yards from the site of Whitehall Palace, will bring you to the country's finest group of royal buildings, not the Tudor towers, turrets and gables of her birthplace, but their splendid successors, built by Sir Christopher Wren and Inigo Jones.

Beached alongside is the **Cutty Sark** (Monday–Saturday, 10.30am –5pm; Sunday, noon–5pm; noon–6pm, April–September), that greyhound of clippers that carried China tea and, later, Australian

The Royal Naval College

wool from her launch in Scotland in 1869 to her retirement in 1922 – the last and the fastest. The article of underwear worn by the lady on the prow is a Scottish nightshirt, a 'cutty sark'. The clipper (pictured right) now carries a cargo of a collection of superb figureheads, memorials of a vanished fleet.

Dwarfed in size, though not in terms of achievement, is **Gipsy Moth IV** (Monday–Saturday, 11am–6pm; Sunday, 2.30–6pm; closed Winter). In 1966–7 Sir Francis Chichester was the first to sail single-handed round the world in this ketch in 226 days, covering 29,630 miles (47,685km). Nearby is the entrance to the Foot Tunnel which leads to the Isle of Dogs (nerve centre of the new Docklands development). After a cold, damp trudge through the tunnel you are rewarded by an unsurpassed view of Greenwich, the 'Queen's View', from the other side. If you are interested in London's new city, take the Docklands Light Railway: it runs around and over much of the innovative new sites.

Back by the pier on the Greenwich side, the riverside walk passes the two blocks of the **Royal Naval College**, with a gap between to ensure the Queen's unobstructed view of the river from Queen's House, and ends by the Regency **Trafalgar Tavern**, where Cabinet Ministers came for whitebait dinners. Continue ahead past the Yacht, the Trinity Almshouses, founded in 1613, and the power station, to **Union Wharf**. It is like coming to a clearing in the forest. Lunch, with good views of Greenwich Reach, can be had at the **Cutty Sark** pub, which looks as if it was built of ships' timbers.

Back at Park Row, cross Romney Road to the **National Maritime Museum** (Monday–Saturday, 10am–6pm; Sunday 2–5pm). A colonnaded walk links the west and east wings with the **Queen's House** on the line of the old Dover Road, which tunnels beneath Inigo Jones's building, England's first Palladian villa. It was intended for James I's Queen Anne, but not completed until after her death by Charles I for Henrietta Maria. Tiptoe through the beauty of the wrought-iron balustrade on the Tulip Staircase. Leave by the colonnade for the west wing and the **Neptune Hall**, where sail gives way to steam and oar-power. The Royal Barge of 1732, built to Kent's design and carved by Richards, the King's Carver, is a riot of lions, dragons and scaly monsters.

From the Romney Road exit turn right in King William Walk into the **Royal Naval College** (Friday–Wednesday, 2.30–5pm; Thursday, 2.30–4.45pm), which occupies the site of the Tudor Palace. Here, Cromwell's sense of history appears to have deserted him. During the Commonwealth he allowed it to serve as a biscuit factory for his troops in Scotland. Not until 1694 was Wren ap-

proached to design, not a palace, but a hospital for elderly and sick seamen. The Royal Naval College came here fròm Portsmouth in 1873, so only the Painted Hall in King William Block and the Chapel in Queen Mary Block are open to view. The splendour of the architecture is matched by Thornhill's decoration of the **Painted Hall**, which was begun in 1707, but not completed until 1726. The **Chapel** dates from 1742, but was rebuilt by James 'Athenian' Stuart after an extensive fire.

Opposite the entrance to the College is the **Covered Market**, now given over to arts and crafts. Where St Alfege's church puts on a bold front to the street, turn left past Greenwich Theatre, a phoenix risen from the shell of an old music hall, into Croom's Hill. Among its fine 17th- and 18th-century houses is a Wren-style gazebo of 1672. Keep left along Chesterfield Walk for the **Ranger's House** (daily, February–October, 10am–5pm; November–January, 10am–4pm), once the home of Lord Chesterfield: portraits downstairs and the Dolmetsch Collection of musical instruments above.

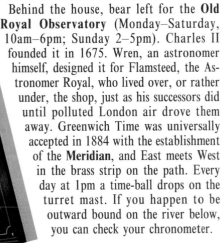

Behind the house, bear left for the **Old Royal Observatory** (Monday–Saturday, 10am–6pm; Sunday 2–5pm). Charles II founded it in 1675. Wren, an astronomer himself, designed it for Flamsteed, the Astronomer Royal, who lived over, or rather under, the shop, just as his successors did until polluted London air drove them away. Greenwich Time was universally accepted in 1884 with the establishment of the **Meridian**, and East meets West in the brass strip on the path. Every day at 1pm a time-ball drops on the turret mast. If you happen to be outward bound on the river below, you can check your chronometer.

Hampton Court Palace

By river or train to the great 16th-century palace of Hampton Court; get lost in the maze, and see the splendour in which Cardinal Wolsey and Henry VIII passed their days.

—Hampton Court Station on the Suburban Line from Waterloo; or boat trip from Westminster Pier (Easter–October. Tel: 071-930 2062 for times)—

From the Landing Stage a short path leads to the moat bridge, but the best approach is through the **Trophy Gates** (mid-March–mid-October, 9.30am–6pm; mid-October–mid-March, 9.30am–4.30pm). Here the scale and complexity of the great Tudor palace with its forest of chimneys and turrets is at its most impressive, but this is only one side of the coin. Behind lies Sir Christopher Wren's contribution, which invites comparison with Versailles.

Cardinal Wolsey, the butcher's son who rose to the highest offices in the Church, with a town house in Whitehall which later became a palace, bought the manor in 1514 and built himself a country seat at Hampton of such magnificence as to raise the envy of Henry VIII. Too late, Wolsey offered it to him as a sweetener, only to have all his possessions taken from him. A year after being charged with treason he was dead. Wolsey's **Great Gatehouse**, originally two storeys higher, rises over a dry moat and a bridge built by Henry VIII, and only excavated in recent times. Charles II had 'improved' them out of existence! **Base Court** is all Wolsey and built of plummy red brick. Behind the mullioned windows are the 280 rooms he kept prepared for guests. The medallions were made by

Giovanni da Majano – eight for a 1521 pound! The stone roof of **Anne Boleyn's Gateway** has Henry and Anne's initials in lovers' knots, not, unhappily, recording a very lasting state of affairs.

In **Clock Court** is the Astronomical Clock made by Nicholas Oursian in 1540. Henry's **Great Hall** fills one side of the court; at its end, possibly the finest example in England of an oriel window. On the south side is Wren's colonnade, as contrasting to the Tudor as the glass pyramid to the Louvre. To complete this trip through time, the east side with the gateway was remodelled by William Kent in 1732 in his own idea of revived Gothic. Wolsey's and Henry's buildings bring a nice domestic feel to the north range of the palace. It is somehow easier to catch the spirit of the time in the **Wine Cellar** and the **Kitchens**, where serving places, stairs and the Horn Room separated them from table in the Great Hall. There Shakespeare and his Company of Players may well have entertained

Queen Elizabeth I. Our only view of the **Chapel Royal** is from the Royal Pew or Oratory, where Henry VIII heard Mass oblivious of piercing screams from his wife Catherine Howard in the nearby gallery. After her death, a figure in white and unearthly shrieks gained it the title of the Haunted Gallery. It is something of a relief to turn to the **Wolsey Rooms**, and his sitting room in particular with its small scale, beautiful decoration and panelling.

Fountain Court reflects Wren's intention to rebuild the whole palace for William and Mary. Begun in 1685, only the east and south fronts were completed. The grandeur is somehow lacking, but you can relate to Hampton Court where Versailles intimidates. Grand staircases lead to the **State Rooms**, richly ornamented with Verrio's painting, Gibbons's carving, Tijou's ironwork and incomparable pictures. Among other delights is Wren's **Banqueting House**, William's summer eating place. Exquisitely fine carving from Gibbons: the **Great Vine** can still astonish after more than 200 years, and the **Maze** defy every solution. As Harris said in *Three Men in a Boat*, 'We'll just walk round for ten minutes and then go and get some lunch.' Be advised, have some lunch first. The **Tiltyard Restaurant** is nearby or, in Hampton Court Road opposite the Trophy Gates, are pubs like the **Charlton Hotel** and **Cardinal Wolsey**. Wren spent the rest of his life in sight of the palace at Old Court House.

Return to the pier for a Richmond boat, or cross the bridge to the railway station for Waterloo.

Calendar of Special Events

Specific dates for many of the following events vary from year to year. The London Tourist Board will be able to provide more detailed information (071-730 3488).

January

New Year's Day Parade from Berkeley Square to Hyde Park.
World Doubles Tennis Championships, Royal Albert Hall.
London International Boat Show, Earl's Court.
Charles I Commemoration (last Sunday): English Civil War Society dress up as Royalists and march along Whitehall.

February

Crufts Dog Show, Earl's Court: the most coveted canine prize.
Accession Day, opposite Dorchester Hotel, Hyde Park: a 41-gun salute to mark the anniversary of the Queen's accession to the throne.
Chinese New Year: colourful Chinese celebrations centring around Gerrard Street in Chinatown.

Valentine's Day: annual day for lovers on the 14th.
Shrove Tuesday (41 days before Easter): the day before Lent is traditionally celebrated with pancakes.

March

Ideal Home Exhibition, Earl's Court.
Oxford and Cambridge Boat Race: annual race between university oarsmen on the Thames between Putney and Mortlake.
Chelsea Antiques Fair, Old Town Hall, King's Road SW3.
Easter Parade, Battersea Park: carnival with floats and fancy dress costumes (starts 3pm).
Camden Jazz Festival, Camden Town: includes jazz, opera, dance, film and exhibitions.

April

April Fool's Day (1 April): throughout the morning Britons go out of their way to trick each other.
London Harness Horse Parade, Regent's Park: horses parade in harness around the inner circle.
London Marathon, Greenwich Park: one of the world's largest with a route

from Greenwich Park to Westminster.
Queen's Birthday (21 April): the occasion of the Queen's real birthday is celebrated with a gun salute in Hyde Park and at the Tower of London.
London Book Fair, at the Barbican.

May

Chelsea Flower Show, at the Royal Hospital sw3.
Royal Windsor Horse Show, Windsor Great Park.
Beating the Retreat, Horse Guards Parade, Whitehall: ceremonial display of military bands.
FA Cup Final, Wembley: final of the nation's main football competition.
Oak Apple Day, Chelsea Royal Hospital: parade of Chelsea pensioners in memory of their founder, Charles II.

June

Derby Day, Epsom Racecourse: famous flat race for three-year-old colts and fillies.
Royal Academy Summer Exhibition, Burlington House, Piccadilly: large exhibition of work by professional and amateur artists (until August).
Trooping the Colour, Horse Guards Parade: the Queen's 'official' birthday celebrations with a ceremonial parade of regimental colours.
Royal Ascot: elegant and dressy race meeting attended by royalty.
Grosvenor House Antiques Fair, Grosvenor House Hotel, Park Lane.
Wimbledon Lawn Tennis Championships: the year's sporting highlight.

July

Henley Royal Regatta, Henley on Thames: international rowing regatta.
Henry Wood Promenade Concerts, Royal Albert Hall: series of classical concerts known as 'The Proms'.
Royal Tournament, Earl's Court: dis-

plays from the Armed Forces.
Swan Upping on the Thames: officials row up and down registering all the swans on the Thames.
Doggett's Coat and Badge Race, London Bridge: traditional race for single scull boats between London Bridge and Chelsea.

August

Notting Hill Carnival, Ladbroke Grove (bank holiday weekend): colourful West Indian street carnival (the largest in Europe).
London Riding Horse Parade, Rotton Row, Hyde Park: competition for the best turned out horse and rider.
International Street Performers' Festival, Covent Garden piazza.

September

Chelsea Antiques Fair, Old Town Hall, King's Road sw3.
Horseman's Sunday, Church of St John & St Michael, w2: service dedicated to the horse, with mounted vicar and congregation.

Notting Hill Carnival

Guy Fawkes Night (fifth): firework celebrations in many of London's parks of Guy Fawkes's failure to blow up the Houses of Parliament in 1605.
Remembrance Sunday (nearest to the 11th): commemorates those lost at war with the main wreath-laying service at the Cenotaph, Whitehall.
State Opening of Parliament, House of Lords, Westminster: the Queen officially reopens Parliament following the summer recess.
Christmas Lights: switched on in Oxford and Regent streets.

December

Olympia International Horse Show, Olympia Exhibition Centre
Christmas Carol Services, Trafalgar Square.
January Sales: they begin earlier each year.
Christmas holiday: 24 December–2 January.
New Year's Eve, Trafalgar Square: thousands congregate for a midnight celebration.

Opposite: Guy Fawkes Night
Below: Costermongers' Festival

October

Costermongers' Pearly Harvest Festival, Church of St Martin-in-the-Fields, Trafalgar Square (first Sunday): Pearly Kings and Queens from London's Cockney community attend this service in their traditional suits and frocks covered with pearl buttons.
Judges' Service: the British legal year begins with a procession of judges in full attire from Westminster Abbey to the Houses of Parliament.
Horse of the Year Show, Wembley.
Trafalgar Day Parade: commemorates Nelson's victory at Trafalgar.
Motor Show, Earl's Court.

November

London to Brighton Veteran Car Run (first Sunday): hundreds of veteran cars and their proud owners start out sedately from Hyde Park.
Lord Mayor's Show: grand procession from the Guildhall in the City to the Royal Courts of Justice, celebrating the Mayor's election.

What to know!
Practical Information

Arriving

From Heathrow Airport the simplest way to reach central London is via the Underground, on the Piccadilly Line. It takes 45 minutes and costs £3. By coach you can take the London Regional Transport red double-decker Airbus service. It picks up from all terminals leaving at half hourly intervals between 6.30am and 10.15pm

daily and costs £5 one way. The A1 bus goes to Victoria, via Earl's Court and Knightsbridge, whilst the A2 bus goes to Russell Square, via Marble Arch and Baker Street. For 24-hour Airbus information, call 081-668 7261. At non rush-hour times, the Airbus can be faster than the Underground. A ride in a black cab will cost upwards of £30, but is the fastest and most direct method.

Gatwick Airport is served by main-line 'Gatwick Express' train and coach services into London, both running to and from Victoria. The train leaves every 15 minutes from 5.30am–10pm; otherwise every hour around the clock. It takes just half an hour and costs £8.60 one way. Flightline 777 coaches leave from both the North and South terminals and take about 70 minutes to reach Victoria. A single fare is £8 (US and Canadian dollars accepted).

London's subsidiary airports are Luton, Stansted and London City. Luton Airport is served with a regular train service to Luton Station, and thereby to London, taking 45 minutes, and the District 757 coach service to Victoria taking 70 minutes. The better train service is from Luton to King's Cross Thameslink.

From Stansted Airport there are direct trains which run regularly to Liverpool Street station. National Express run a coach service connecting Heathrow, Gatwick, Stansted and Luton airports with each other and Victoria. Enquiries on 071-730 0202.

London City Airport is badly served by transport despite its close proximity to the city (6 miles/10km) with the options of a taxi, or a bus to the nearest tube station (Plaistow). Unfortunately the river bus service which used to serve the airport is no longer in operation.

Airport Information
GATWICK AIRPORT, 0293 535353.
HEATHROW AIRPORT, 081-759 4321.
LONDON CITY AIRPORT, 071-474 5555.
LUTON AIRPORT, 0582 405100.
STANSTED AIRPORT, 0279 680500.

Passports
Passport holders from most European countries, the Americas, South Africa, Japan, and most Commonwealth countries do not generally require a visa to enter the UK for a short stay. If in any doubt check with the British Embassy in your home country before you leave.

Customs
Duty free allowances have recently changed. Long-haul travellers coming from outside Europe can bring in the following: 1 litre of spirits or 2 litres of wine (plus an extra 2 litres of table wine if no spirits are purchased); 200 cigarettes or 100 cigarillos, or 30 cigars, or 250g of tobacco; 60cc perfume or 250cc toilet water; gifts or other goods up to an ungenerous maximum value of £32.

It is prohibited to bring animals, plants, perishable foods, certain drugs, firearms and obscene material into the country without prior arrangement. There are no restrictions on the amount of foreign or British currency which can be brought into the UK.

Climate
London winters are cold and blustery, but snowfall is rare in the city, whilst in summer months, particularly July and August, temperatures can reach above 80°F (27°C). The weather is unpredictable and temperatures can fluctuate considerably from day to day with surprise showers catching people unawares all year round. Come prepared with wet weather clothes and dress in 'removable layers' whatever the season. For recorded weather information, call 0891-141214.

Time
British Summer Time (BST) begins in March when the nation puts its clocks forward one hour and ends in October when clocks go back to Greenwich Mean Time (GMT). Consult newspapers and British diaries for dates.

Public Holidays
New Year's Day, Good Friday, Easter Monday, May Day (first Monday in May), Spring Bank Holiday (last Monday in May), August Bank Holiday (last Monday in August), Christmas Day, Boxing Day.

Electricity
The electrical current in the UK is 240 Volts. Most hotels have 110-Volt shaving sockets.

Travelcards

The Travelcard is a one-day pass that allows unlimited travel on the Tube, buses, Docklands Light Railway and British Rail's Network SouthEast for £3.70 (all zones). The Travelcard can be used after 9.30am on weekdays and all day Saturday, Sunday, and public holidays and is readily available from all Underground and Network SouthEast stations.

Travelcards are also available for a week (£29.50 all zones) or for a month (£113.30 all zones) and can be used at any time. To buy a week- or month-long card you will need to supply a passport-sized photograph.

Taxis

London's famous black cabs are licensed and display the strictly regulated charges on a meter. Their drivers are well trained, having had to complete a rigorous study of the capital's streets (acquiring 'The Knowledge') before being able to take to the road. Minicabs are not allowed to compete with black cabs on the streets and must be hired by telephone or from a kiosk. Make sure you agree upon a fee beforehand and, unlike black cabs, don't expect them to know precise destinations.

On the River

Boat trips are an excellent way to see many of London's sights. Westminster Passenger Services Federation run a riverboat service between Hampton Court (upriver) and the Westminster Pier. Catamaran Cruisers operate downstream to Greenwich from Charing Cross Pier. Services vary from summer to winter with downriver services tending to run all year round (10.30am–4pm), whilst most upriver services only run between April and October. There are piers at Richmond, Kew, Putney, Westminster, Charing Cross, London Bridge, the Tower and

GETTING AROUND

The Underground (also known as the Tube) is the quickest way to get around London. It runs between 5.30am and midnight, and is extremely busy in the rush hours (8–9.30am and 5–6.30pm). Ensure you have a valid ticket and keep hold of it after you have passed through the electronic barriers as it is illegal to travel without one. Fares are based upon a zone system. Smoking is prohibited.

The Docklands Light Railway, which opened in 1987, is an excellent way to see the modern re-development of London's old dock area. A fully automated system, it has two branches running from Bank and Stratford to Island Gardens (on the Isle of Dogs), and runs in the same way as the Tube. However, the whole system is currently being extended, causing some disruption to services.

London buses provide a comprehensive service throughout Greater London and have their route and number clearly displayed on the front. Unlike the Underground, buses carry on running on certain routes hourly throughout the night, centring on Trafalgar Square.

Greenwich. Both Westminster Passenger Services and Catamaran Cruisers run several special services, including the circular cruises, floodlight and supper cruises. For more information, call Westminster on 071-930 2062, and Catamaran on 071-839 3572.

Driving

In the UK, drive on the left and observe the speed limits: 30mph (50kph) in urban areas, 60mph (96kph) on A roads away from built-up areas and 70mph (112kph) on motorways and dual carriageways. It is illegal to drink and drive and penalties are severe. The law also states that drivers and passengers must wear seat-belts where available. Cars should give way to pedestrians at zebra crossings.

Driving in London, with its maze of one-way streets, impatient drivers, congestion and parking problems, can be a nightmare. Parking is a major headache in central London. Meters are slightly cheaper than car parks, but only allow parking for a maximum of two hours. If using a meter, don't leave your car parked a moment longer than your time allows and do not return and insert more money once your time has run out. These are offences for which you can face a fine in the region of £30 and there are plenty of traffic wardens ready to give out tickets. Meter parking is free after 6.30pm each evening, after 1.30pm in most areas on Saturday afternoon and all day Sunday. However, always check the details given on the meter so as not to be caught out.

Don't ever leave your car on a double yellow line or in areas reserved for residents and permit holders, as you are liable to have your wheels clamped or your car towed away and face an exceptionally heavy fine as well as considerable inconvenience.

Car Rental

To rent a car in Britain you should be over 21 years old and have held a valid full driving licence for more than one year.

The cost of hiring a car will usually include insurance and unlimited mileage. It does not, however, include insurance cover for accidental damage to interior trim, wheels and tyres or insurance for other drivers without prior approval. It can be worth shopping around before deciding on a car as some companies offer special weekend and holiday rates.

Car Rental Companies
AVIS, 081-848 8733.
EUROPCAR, 0345-222525.
HERTZ RENT-A-CAR, 081-679 1799.
EURODOLLAR, 0895-233300.

24-hour Petrol Stations
SHELL, 104 Bayswater Road W2.
TEXACO, 71 King's Cross Road WC1.
MOBIL, 83 Park Lane W1.
BP, 104 Finchley Road NW3.
ESSO, 87 Goldhawk Road W12.

24-hour Car Parks:
Park Lane W1 (the largest in central London).
Brewer Street W1.
Newport Place WC2.
Upper St Martin's Lane WC2.

24-hour Breakdown Assistance
AA, 0800 887766.
RAC, 0800 828282.
NATIONAL BREAKDOWN, 0800 400600.

NATIONAL TRUST, 071-222 9251.
EVENTS FOR CHILDREN IN LONDON, 0591-505456.
SPORTSLINE, 0891-505442.

TOURIST INFORMATION

London's official tourist board is the London Tourist Board (LTB). At the following tourist information centres the LTB provides general information and booking services for hotels, theatre and sightseeing tours: Victoria Station, Heathrow Terminals 1,2,3 (Underground station concourse), Selfridges and Liverpool Street Station. For information prior to your visit, write to the London Tourist Board, 26 Grosvenor Gardens, Victoria, London SW1W 0DU, allowing them reasonable time to reply. Information by telephone is on a pre-recorded message. The English Tourist Board is at Thames Tower, Black's Road, London W6 9EL. Tel: 081-846 9000.

London Regional Transport provide tourist information centres at the following Underground stations: Victoria, Piccadilly Circus, Oxford Circus, Euston, Liverpool Street and King's Cross.

The British Travel Centre at 12 Regent Street W1 provides comprehensive travel, accommodation, entertainment and sightseeing information and booking services for the whole of Britain. Open 9am–6.30pm Monday–Friday; 10am–4pm Saturday and Sunday.

Information by Phone

LTB, 0891-505 440.
LONDON REGIONAL TRANSPORT (24 hours), 071-222 1234.
RIVER INFORMATION, 0839-123432.
ARTSLINE, arts information for the disabled, 071-388 2227.

MONEY MATTERS

Banks are open 9.30am–4/4.30pm Monday–Friday, and some also open on Saturday morning. The major banks (Lloyds, Barclays, Midland and National Westminster) can be found on most high streets and tend to offer similar exchange rates. They charge no commission on travellers' cheques presented in sterling or for changing a cheque in another currency if the bank is connected to your own bank at home. However, there will be a charge for changing cash into another currency or for giving cash against a credit card. There are automatic tellers outside most banks where appropriate credit or cashpoint cards can be used to obtain cash.

Money may also be changed by travel agents, such as Thomas Cook, and at some large department stores. There are also numerous Bureaux de Change throughout London, but you should be wary of changing money at these as they may rip you off. If you do have to use one, try to ensure it's carrying the LTB code of conduct sticker. Chequepoint is a more reputable chain with 24-hour branches at Piccadilly Circus, Leicester Square, Marble Arch, Bayswater and Victoria Underground stations.

Credit cards are widely accepted in shops, hotels and restaurants in London, although you should watch out for the few exceptions. Eurocheques are becoming more widely accepted.

Tipping

Good service in restaurants and hotels and from cab drivers, hairdressers, porters and sightseeing guides should be rewarded with a tip of not less than 10 per cent. Tipping any other service has to be gauged carefully as in some cases it may offend. It is not customary to tip in bars and pubs, theatres and cinemas. Hotels and restaurants may add a 10–15 per cent service charge to your bill which should be specified on the tariff. If you have justifiable reason to be dissatisfied, you may deduct this.

Business Hours

Shop and office hours in London are usually 9am–5.30pm Monday–Saturday. Shops in the centre of town rarely close for lunch and may stay open later, particularly around Covent Garden and Piccadilly Circus. Very few shops are open on Sunday apart from newsagents, small grocery shops and large warehouse stores away from the centre. Late-night shopping, until as late as 8pm, is on Thursday in Oxford and Regent Streets and on Wednesday in Knightsbridge and Kensington.

COMMUNICATION

Recent years have seen considerable changes to London's public telephones with the sad replacement of the traditional red call box with modern glass-and-stainless-steel booths. There are now two separate telephone companies: British Telecom (BT) and Mercury. BT public telephones are more plentiful and make no charge for service calls. Mercury's are reputedly cheaper for international calls, but their striking blue-and-grey call boxes are less prevalent than BT's. In addition to coin call boxes, both companies provide telephones that will only accept plastic phone cards (resembling credit cards), widely available from post offices and newsagents for varying amounts between £1 and £20. Mercury phones will also accept major credit cards for which there is a minimum

charge of 50p, a service which BT too is gradually introducing.

In 1990 the London 01 changed to 071 for inner London and 081 for outer London. These codes must be used when calling one area of London from another and when dialling from anywhere else in the UK.

International Calls

To dial other countries first dial the international access code 010, then the country code: Australia (61); France (33); Germany (49); Italy (39); Japan (81); Netherlands (31); Spain (34); US and Canada (1). If using a US credit phone card, dial the company's access number below – Sprint, Tel: 0800 89 0877; AT&T, Tel: 0800 89 0011; MCI, Tel: 0800 89 0222.

Useful Numbers

Emergency, police, fire and ambulance, dial 999.

The Operator (for technical difficulties), 100.

Directory Enquiries, 192.

The International Operator, 155.

The Speaking Clock, 123

Postal Services

Post offices are open Monday–Friday, 9am–5pm; Saturday, 9am–noon.

Stamps are available from post offices, or from vending machines outside, and from some newsagents and shops. It costs 25p to send a letter first class in the UK, 19p for second

class. To send a postcard to an EC destination costs 25p, 30p to the rest of Europe and 41p worldwide.

London's main post office is at Trafalgar Square, situated on the east side near the church of St Martin-in-the-Fields and is open 8am–8pm Monday–Saturday.

HEALTH & EMERGENCIES

In an absolute emergency call 999 for fire, ambulance or police. Otherwise, call Directory Enquiries on 192 and ask for the number of the nearest police station, hospital casualty department, or the number of your country's embassy in London. Unless you come from an EC country or your country has reciprocal arrangements with the UK, you will be liable for the cost of medical treatment and should therefore have adequate health insurance before you arrive.

GREAT CHAPEL STREET MEDICAL CENTRE *13 Great Chapel Street W1 (071-437 9360),* is a National Health Service clinic with afternoon surgery Monday–Friday where anyone can walk in off the street without an appointment.
Emergency dental care call 081-677 6363 or Eastman's Dental Hospital on 071-915 1000.
Chemists: Boots is a large chain of

pharmacies with numerous branches throughout London that will make up prescriptions. The branch at 114 Queensway W2 is open until 10pm daily whilst Bliss Chemist at Marble Arch is open until midnight daily.

LOST PROPERTY

For possessions lost on buses or the Tube, contact London Transport Lost Property Office, 200 Baker Street NW1 (071-486 2496) 9.30am–2pm Monday–Friday. The Taxi Lost Property Office is at 15 Penton Street N1 (071-833 0996).

Left Luggage
Most main railway stations have left luggage departments where you can leave your suitcases on a short-term basis, and/or provide lockers in which items can be left for 24 hours. These offices open around 7am and close at 10.30pm with the exception of Euston (open 24 hours). Paddington has no left-luggage facilities.

MEDIA

Newspapers and Magazines
The quality national daily newspapers are *The Times* and the *Daily Telegraph* (right bias), *The Guardian* (left bias) and *The Independent* (centre). There are also the *Financial Times* and the weekly *European*. Tabloids such as *The Sun*, *The Star* and *The Mirror* are smaller with news issues swamped by pages of gossip. More up-market, but still gossipy are the *Daily Mail*, *Daily Express* and *Today*. Most of these papers publish a Sunday edition with a colour supplement.

For information listings on entertainment and events in London, consult the weekly magazine *Time Out*, published every Wednesday. London's local paper is the *Evening Standard* which comes out on weekday afternoons. Although it covers major international news, it is mainly concerned with events and information relating to the capital, and also contains extensive classified advertisements. Foreign newspapers and magazines can be found at the following newsagents:

JOHN MENZIES, 104 Long Acre WC2.

CAPITAL NEWSAGENTS, 48 Old Compton Street W1.

A MORONI & SON, 68 Old Compton Street W1.

SELFRIDGES, Oxford Street W1.

W H SMITHS Most large city centre branches and outlets at many railway stations.

Television

Britain has four major television channels: BBC1, BBC2, ITV and CHANNEL 4. They have a reputation for broadcasting some of the best quality television in the world. However, with the advent of satellite television and independent television franchising, things are forecast to change in the future as stations become ever more commercially motivated and biased towards mass audience programmes such as soap operas, game shows and comedies. The two British Broadcasting Corporation channels (BBC1 & BBC2) do not rely on advertising for financial support as do the independent channels, ITV and CHANNEL 4. BBC2 broadcasts more cultural and serious programmes than BBC1 whilst CHANNEL 4 is less mainstream and more pioneering than ITV, commissioning films and broadcasting programmes of specialist interest. Recent years have seen an epidemic of satellite dishes appearing on houses throughout the country, providing TV addicts with 24-hour news, music, films and sporting events courtesy of British Sky Broadcasting. Cable television is a popular alternative to satellite, with more channels to chose from.

Radio

Many new independent stations have sprung up in recent years. However, the BBC still continues to dominate the British airwaves with:

RADIO 1, 98.8FM, mainly pop.

RADIO 2, 89.2FM, easy-listening.

RADIO 3, 91.3FM, classical music.

RADIO 4, 93.5FM, news, current affairs, consumer affairs and drama.

RADIO 5, 909MW, general interest.

GLR (Greater London Radio) 94.9FM, for the more mature listener.

London's most popular independent stations are:

CAPITAL RADIO 95.8FM, 24-hour-pop.

CAPITAL GOLD 1548AM, 24-hour golden oldies.

LBC NEWSTALK 97.3FM, news, discussion and phone-ins.

Jazz FM 102.2FM, 24-hour jazz.

Kiss FM 100FM, 24-hour dance.

ACCOMMODATION

London's hotels are expensive with prices generally higher than anywhere else in Europe. However, cost does not always mean quality, so look out for the LTB membership sticker indicating that certain standards have been met, and always try to view rooms before booking. A tax of 17.5 per cent and service are usually included in the price of a room; this

should be clearly stated on the tariff. Tipping is at the guest's discretion.

In the height of the summer season (April–September) it is advisable to book before you arrive. The London Tourist Board provide a bed booking service through their information centres or by telephone (credit cards only): call 071-824 8844.

The hotels listed below are located centrally and have been chosen, as far as possible, for providing welcoming English hospitality in pleasent surroundings or for their excellent location. The best areas for moderately priced bed and breakfast accommodation are Victoria, Knightsbridge, Earl's Court, Bayswater and Bloomsbury. However, many of the moderately priced hotels are small and don't have restaurants, although some have room service. It is often well worth calling into the more expensive hotels for afternoon tea or cocktails.

Some hotels offer babysitting and booking services for theatres and restaurants, whilst smarter hotels are geared up for business travellers with conference, fax and copying facilities.

Many hotels, even the Ritz and the Savoy, offer specially discounted weekend rates depending on the season, often with extra incentives such as guided tours and champagne.

Prices quoted are for the minimum cost of bed and breakfast per room with two people sharing.

Luxury (over £150)

THE BEAUFORT
33 Beaufort Gardens SW3 (071-584 5252. Fax 071-589 2834). Excellent small hotel in an elegant Knightsbridge square which works hard to maintain its fine reputation. Guests are given a front door key and invited to help themselves to drinks and food (room service menu) and have use of a nearby health club, all included in the

room price. The pastel rooms are filled with extras such as a decanter of brandy, Swiss chocolates, fruit, flowers and even an umbrella. From *£160.*

BROWN'S
Dover Street W1 (071-493 6020. Fax 071-493 9381). Opened in 1837 by James Brown, former manservant to Lord Byron, this distinguished Mayfair hotel has expanded into 14 Georgian houses. Renowned for impeccable service and a traditional country house atmosphere, it is magnificently furnished with rich wood panelling and antiques. 120 rooms. *£230.*

THE BERKELEY
Wilton Place SW1 (071-235 6000. Fax 071-235 4330). Deluxe Knightsbridge hotel which is considered to be one of Britain's finest. Refined, with period detailing from the old Berkeley, which was formerly in Piccadilly before moving here in 1972. Rooms are comfortably furnished in a traditional English style, some with terraces. There is a Roman bath-style roof-top pool, gymnasium and sauna. *£250.*

BLAKE'S
33 Roland Gardens SW7 (071-370 6701. Fax 071-373 0442). Notable for its alternative style, this exotic hotel is popular with those involved in the entertainment industries. Laid back, with more than a hint of the 1970s, this unique hotel is the creation of actress and interior designer, Anouska Hempel. 52 rooms. *£165.*

THE CAPITAL
Basil Street SW3 (071-589 5171. Fax 071-225 0011). Intimate town house in the heart of Knightsbridge. Relaxed and comfortable with courteous service and *fin de siècle* elegance. Restaurant has one Michelin star and serves fine French cuisine. The 54 rooms are tastefully furnished. *£190.*

THE GORING

15 Beeston Place SW1 (071-396 9000. Fax 071-834 4393). Just behind Buckingham Palace is this gracious hotel, run by the Goring family since 1910 when it was the first hotel in the world to have a bathroom and central heating in every room. 86 rooms decorated in a dignified fashion. *£165.*

THE RITZ

Piccadilly W1 (071-493 8181. Fax 071-493 2687). Lavish hotel with overtones of sheer decadence; synonymous with class and style the world over. Timeless, memorable and expensive. 130 rooms. *£210.*

Expensive (£150 and under)

THE ABBEY COURT

20 Pembridge Gardens W2 (071-221 7518. Fax 071-792 0858). Commendable hotel in a beautifully restored town house where great attention is paid to detail. Rooms are delightfully furnished in English country style, all with Italian marble bathrooms with whirlpool baths. 22 rooms. *£120.*

THE BASIL STREET HOTEL

Knightsbridge SW3 (071-581 3311. Fax 071-581 3693). Old-fashioned hotel with plenty of English country charm. Built in 1910, it is privately owned and attracts a regular clientele from amongst the gentry. Rooms are traditional and comfortable. Excellent services. 94 rooms. *£166.*

THE CADOGAN

Sloane Street SW1 (071-235 7141. Fax 071-245 0994). This fine Edwardian building was once home to actress and society beauty, Lillie Langtry. Old-fashioned elegance has been combined with modern comforts. Rooms are individually decorated in a classic style. *£150.*

THE COBURG

Bayswater Road W2 (071-221 2217. Fax 071-229 0557). Recently restored to its former glory, this luxury purpose-built Edwardian hotel overlooks Kensington Palace and gardens. With an atmosphere of calm and comfort. 132 rooms. *£95.*

THE RUBENS

Buckingham Palace Road, Victoria SW1 (071-834 6600. Fax 071-828 5401). Ideally situated opposite the Royal Mews, close to Buckingham Palace, this smartly modernised hotel is decorated in pastel shades with elegant new furniture. A high traditional standard of service. 189 rooms. *£132.*

TOWER THISTLE HOTEL

St Katharine's Way E1 (071-481 2575. Fax 071-488 4106). What this large modern hotel lacks in charm is compensated for by its breathtaking location. On the bank of the Thames, it is surrounded by The Tower of London, Tower Bridge, and St Katharine's Dock. Also handy for the City, it has all the luxuries. 808 rooms. *£145.*

Moderate (£100 and under)

THE ACADEMY HOTEL

17–21 Gower Street WC1 (071-631 4115. Fax 071-636 3442). Located within two nicely converted Georgian town houses in the heart of literary Bloomsbury. The dining room is 1980s design whilst the rooms are more traditionally furnished. Patio garden. 33 rooms, most with private facilities. *£95.*

THE CLAVERLEY

13–14 Beaufort Gardens SW3 (071-589 8541. Fax 071-584 3410). Respected Knightsbridge hotel offering traditional English hospitality. Furnished in quaint English country style with Laura Ashley and Chesterfield sofas. 30 individually styled rooms, many with bathrooms. *£100.*

DURRANT'S HOTEL
George Street W1 (071-935 8131. Fax 071-487 3510). Located just north of Oxford Street; discreet family-run hotel with the feeling of a country inn. Public rooms furnished with old wood panelling. Bedrooms recently renovated in feminine styles. Well priced for the area. 96 rooms. *£105.*

HAZLITT'S
6 Frith Street W1 (071-434 1771. Fax 071-439 1524). This civilised hotel popular with shyer media celebrities occupies three historic 18th-century town houses in Soho. The 23 rooms, all with bathrooms, are charmingly furnished in classic period style with antiques, plants, and Victorian bath fittings. *£120.*

PORTOBELLO HOTEL
22 Stanley Gardens W11 (071-727 2777. Fax 071-792 9641). Somewhat eccentric, furnished in a hybrid Victorian style, this hotel is close to Portobello's antique market. The 25 rooms, all with private facilities, vary from tiny cabins to unusual suites. Also four-poster suites. *£130.*

WILBRAHAM HOTEL
Wilbraham Place SW1 (071-730 8296. Fax 071-730 6815). Old-fashioned and dated, this privately owned hotel has a distinctively English charm and offers good value in exclusive Belgravia. Convenient for Knightsbridge and Chelsea. 50 bedrooms, mostly with bathrooms. No credit cards. *£70.*

Budget (£60 and under)

ABBEY HOUSE
11 Vicarage Gate W8 (071-727 2594). Inviting budget accommodation within a desirable Kensington street. Furnished in a basic manner, it is well maintained and spruced up annually. 15 rooms. No credit cards. *£52.*

EDEN HOUSE
111 Old Church Street SW3 (071-352 3403). Pleasant town house in a quiet desirable location close to the King's Road. 14 rooms (five family and eight with bath). *£55.*

EDWARD LEAR HOTEL
28–30 Seymour Street W1 (071-402 5401. Fax 071-706 3766). This Georgian house close to Marble Arch was once home to the Victorian painter and poet, Edward Lear. Comfortable and modern. 31 rooms. *£62.*

ELIZABETH HOTEL
37 Eccleston Square SW1 (071-828 6812). Small and friendly private hotel overlooking a grand period square, close to Victoria. Residents have use of private gardens and tennis court. 40 rooms, 32 with bath. *£70.*

FIELDING HOTEL
40 Broad Court, Bow Street WC2 (071-836 8305. Fax 071-497 0064). Covent Garden hotel in a quiet paved street near the Royal Opera House. Small and a bit frayed, it offers a fabulous location at moderate cost. 26 rooms (most with private facilities). *£73.*

THE WILLETT
32 Sloane Gardens, Sloane Square SW1 (071-824 8415. Fax 071-730 4830). Fine small hotel in fashionable neighbourhood. It has been modernised in a tasteful light and airy style. Most of the 19 bedrooms have private facilities. *£80.*

Index

Art & Photo Credits

Photography	**Robert Mort** *and*
92B	**Andrew Eames**
70T	**Courtesy of Harrods**
12, 14	**Courtesy of The Museum of London**
20, 52, 83T, 92T	**Richard T Nowitz**
Cover, 45, 66B, 93	**Spectrum Colour Library**
18, 92T	**Tony Stone Worldwide**
46	**Courtesy of The Tate Gallery**
50B, 70B, 91	**Adam Woolfitt**
Cover Design	**Klaus Geisler**
Cartography	**Berndtson & Berndtson**

UNDERGROUND

Travel Information 071-222-1234
Travelcheck 071-222-1200

© Copyright London Regional Transport

Key to lines

Bakerloo
Central
Circle
District
East London
Hammersmith & City
Jubilee
Metropolitan
Northern
Piccadilly
Victoria
Docklands Light Railway †
Network SouthEast

Restricted service
Peak hours and Sunday mornings
Peak hours only
Peak hours only
Peak hours only
Under construction
Peak hours only

◐ Interchange stations
◯ Connections with British Rail
✦ Connections within walking distance
★ Closed Saturdays and Sundays
✦ Closed Sundays
✦ Served by Piccadilly line early mornings and late evenings Monday to Saturday and all day Sundays
† For opening times see poster journey planners
Certain stations are closed during public holidays

113

INSIGHT GUIDES

INSIGHT *pocket* GUIDES

• •

United States: Houghton Mifflin Company, Boston MA 02108
Tel: (800) 2253362 Fax: (800) 4589501

Canada: Thomas Allen & Son, 390 Steelcase Road East
Markham, Ontario L3R 1G2
Tel: (416) 4759126 Fax: (416) 4756747

Great Britain: GeoCenter UK, Hampshire RG22 4BJ
Tel: (256) 817987 Fax: (256) 817988

Worldwide: Höfer Communications Singapore 2262
Tel: (65) 8612755 Fax: (65) 8616438

❝ **I** was first drawn to the Insight Guides by the excellent "Nepal" volume.
I can think of no book which so effectively captures the essence of a
country. Out of these pages leaped the Nepal I know – the captivating
charm of a people and their culture. I've since discovered and enjoyed
the entire Insight Guide Series. Each volume deals with
a country or city in the same sensitive depth, which is
nowhere more evident than in the superb photography. **❞**

Sir Edmund Hillary